The Chopsticks Diet

The Chopsticks Diet

Japanese-inspired recipes
for easy weight-loss

Kimiko Barber

Photography by Jean Cazals

Kyle Cathie Limited

First published in Great Britain in 2009 by
Kyle Cathie Limited
122 Arlington Road
London, NW1 7HP
www.kylecathie.com

ISBN: 978 1 85626 826 4

A CIP catalogue record for this title is available from the
British Library

10 9 8 7 6 5 4 3 2 1

Text copyright © 2008 by Kimiko Barber
Photographs copyright © 2008 by Jean Cazals
Design copyright © 2008 by Kyle Cathie Limited

Design: Lisa Pettibone
Photography: Jean Cazals
Food stylist: Marie-Ange La Pierre
Props stylist: Wei Tang
Project editor: Sophie Allen
Copy editor: Anna Hitchin
Proofreader: Stephanie Evans
Production: Sha Huxtable

Acknowledgements

My foremost thanks go to Kyle Cathie for commissioning
me to do this book and for all her generous help and kind
encouragement along the way.

Thanks also to Ivan Mulcahy for his reassuring guidance.

Another big thanks to the entire team at Kyle Cathie; the
ever enthusiastic and cheerful Sophie Allen the editor, Wei
Tang props stylist who must have sourced practically every
variety of chopsticks available in London, and the designer
Lisa Pettibone. It has also been huge fun to work with a
French photographer and food stylist team – my special
thanks to Jean Cazals for taking beautiful photographs and
Marie-Ange Lapierre for food styling.

The last but by no means least thanks to my husband,
Stephen.

Ceramics used on pages 81, 87, 98, 136, 141, 153 were
made by the author.

Contents

Introduction

There is only one simple way to lose weight – eat less. We all know this already, so why do we find it difficult to put into practice or to maintain it for a long time? It is because many diet methods involve radical changes to what you can eat and often refer to pre-calculated calories and tables of indices. *The Chopsticks Diet* is straightforward: there are no calorie counts and no tables, but it's full of easy, delicious and healthy Japanese-inspired recipes to eat with chopsticks.

It is a myth that Japanese women don't get fat – there is no such thing as 'slimmer genes' and women in Japan are just as concerned about weight as those of any other nationality. But Japanese women on the whole tend to be slimmer, keep their youthful appearance and enjoy relatively healthy lifestyles for years longer than women in the West. Both Japanese men and women have the longest life expectancies in the world and suffer fewer cardiovascular diseases. Obesity, though, as the Western diet creeps into everyday life, is worryingly on the rise, if still considerably less than in other affluent industrialised nations. It is not what we are but what we eat, how we cook, and how we eat that determines our health and figure.

After having three children in my late thirties, I became and stayed comfortably middle-aged in shape and dressed in baggy clothes to hide my figure. Gone were fashionable skinny dresses and figure-conscious designer suits I loved wearing before, and my wardrobe became colonised by voluminous tent-like dresses, elasticated skirts and baggy trousers. A very poor excuse I know, but it was difficult to go on a diet while my children were small because I cooked s
them, and feeding them often involved eating with them. Worst of all, I ended up picking their leftovers because I felt guilty for wasting food. I then had a grown-ups' supper, often late in the evening with my husband. It was no wonder I put on weight and went up in dress size.

The essence of *The Chopsticks Diet* lies in the Japanese way of food – what they eat and how they eat – exemplified in chopsticks. Since all Japanese food is to be eaten with chopsticks nearly all recipes in this book are designed for eating in this way. Many research findings suggest that eating with chopsticks slows people down and therefore they eat less. It is said that there is as much as a 20 minute time-lag between the stomach becoming full and telling the brain that you are full. Try eating the same amount of food with chopsticks as you would with a knife and fork and you will quickly realise that it is almost impossible. If you eat fast, as most of us do nowadays, your brain cannot accurately monitor the amount of food your stomach is receiving. So it is difficult to know when to stop, therefore we end up eating more than we need. Slow eating is good for you, especially if you want to lose weight.

And take a casual look at the size of portions served in Japanese restaurants and note how small they come. Japanese food is served and presented in small dishes – a diminutive rice or soup bowl sits comfortably in the palm, and small helpings of delicacies from land and sea are arranged in dainty little bowls and saucers – all perfectly designed for eating with chopsticks. There is a saying in Japanese – *hara hachibu* – which means literally that you should eat until you are about 80 per cent satisfied and no more. Leave the table when you are still wishing to eat more but not when you are full.

Eating with chopsticks not only physically slows you down and encourages you to eat less, but it also has the psychological benefit of making you think about the food and the enjoyment you get from it. It naturally requires more concentration than eating with a knife and fork. I prefer using chopsticks, even for non-Japanese food, because it makes me feel more appreciative of food and to me it is a more elegant way of eating. It is interesting to see that today in Japan all school lunches are eaten with chopsticks instead of with an ugly utilitarian invention of the 1960s called a 'spork' (a cross between a spoon and fork) that was intended to make the children eat their tasteless school meals as fast as possible. Japanese children nowadays (who have healthy food prepared for them) are taught to use chopsticks with 'grace' and to make elegant 'chopstick strokes' because we believe that the correct use of chopsticks makes us appreciate food more and increases the pleasure of eating. Among many foody proverbs in Japanese, 'eat with the eyes', seems particularly relevant for explaining the ethos of *The Chopsticks Diet*. I used to think making food look more attractive was intended just for restaurants chefs but the saying also applies to eating. It tells us to take a moment to look and contemplate, and above all, enjoy engaging all five senses of sound, scent, sight, touch and taste of the food.

One of the significant factors that sets the Japanese way of eating apart and makes the nation healthy and slim is the high component of carbohydrate-based energy. In the Japanese diet, carbohydrates, mainly in the form of rice, make up a quarter of the total energy intake. In the West, however, carbohydrate is often portrayed as a villain for slimmers and many diets demonise it. Research shows that the form of energy the body runs on, whether fats, sugar or carbohydrates, makes no difference in losing weight. What matters is the quality of carbohydrate – whether it is 'good' or 'bad' carbohydrate. Good carbohydrate foods are those that are still in their natural state or are still similar to their natural state and not processed. Good carbohydrates are nutritious, and generally high in fibre, giving you more energy and keeping you feeling satisfied for a longer period of time. Fibre-rich foods also help to lower cholesterol levels as well as aiding the body to rid it of its toxins. Traditional Japanese meals feature many good carbohydrate foods such as fresh vegetables, rice, soba noodles, and beans – which all appear extensively in this book. And here is another significant factor that sets Japanese food apart and makes it so healthy and slimming – we don't add fat to our carbohydrates. Rice is delicious to eat on its own and doesn't need additions of fat or sugar like butter or sweet jams. Noodles are cooked in water and eaten with non-fat dashi-based dipping sauce with vegetables. Both rice

and soba noodles are less processed than breads and pasta. Many recipes in the book also feature a number of slimmer-friendly fibre-rich ingredients such as agar-agar, bamboo shoots, burdock, konnyaku, seaweeds and high-vitamin green tea.

There is also no tradition of roasting a large joint of meat in Japanese cooking, indeed many households in Japan still do not have an oven but cook with surface-heat. This is because meat and poultry were forbidden up until the mid-nineteenth century. So this book is full of salads and food that is gently steamed, simmered in flavoursome dashi, grilled or stir-fried using little oil.

But the Japanese are eating more westernised and processed food today than ever before and that is taking its toll on the nation's health. The most striking example is seen in the islands of Okinawa – the archipelago in the South-China Sea, once considered a Shangri-La on the sea, where septuagenarians were regarded mere babies, men and women in their 80s and 90s grew vegetables in their gardens and centenarians were no big deal. Okinawa became the largest American military base in Japan after the end of the Second World War. It took only a few decades to create a different health profile of this one-time health paradise. Okinawans in their 40s and below have grown up on a standard American diet of animal protein especially red meat and highly processed food such as hamburgers, deep-fried potatoes and bread instead of the traditional Okinawan diet of rice, home-grown vegetables and fresh seafood and seaweeds. The health statistics of these younger Okinawans are alarming. Today this Okinawan age group has higher rates of obesity, and a greater risk of cardiovascular disease, liver disease and premature death than the overall Japanese population.

The Chopsticks Diet was conceived while I was writing two Japanese cookbooks back-to-back. I ate the food I tested for the books with chopsticks. I am not expecting you to eat Japanese food with chopsticks everyday for every meal, but I do suggest taking the concept of the book into consideration. Try eating Japanese-inspired food with chopsticks as often as you can – this will be easier to do at home but may be difficult when you eat out. I was so impressed when I once witnessed an Englishman whipping a pair of chopsticks out of his suit pocket in the middle of a very smart restaurant in London to eat mushroom risotto and rocket salad. A classic case of English eccentricity maybe, but when you are eating out in a restaurant or at a friend's house, try emulating chopstick eating – choose less processed food and order more Japanese-like dishes of vegetables and fish and preferably less red meat if possible. In the absence of chopsticks, use a knife and fork with *The Chopsticks Diet* in mind and slow down, cut the food into small pieces, put the knife and fork down between each mouthful and take time to chew and savour the food. You will enjoy the food more that way and the person who has cooked it will be pleased with the care and attention you are paying to their cooking.

Of course eating less food alone does not make you lose weight automatically. Food input is only one side of the equation and you must raise the level of energy output if you want to lose weight. *The Chopsticks Diet* is to help you to eat less and eat healthily, while it is you alone who can control your output of energy, by exercising regularly and maintaining your health and well-being. Taking regular exercise is paramount for keeping fit and shedding weight safely. You will find that the more you eat well the better you feel and the more you enjoy exercise. It is a great cycle of joy in life.

A nice glass of wine adds pleasure to a meal and I am certainly not preaching to you to give up alcohol even while you are trying to lose weight. But if you are wondering why that half stone is refusing to leave you despite healthy and sensible eating and regular exercise – the answer probably lies in your alcohol consumption. Alcohol is second only to fat in the amount of calories it provides but they are 'empty' calories – they won't give you sustainable energies nor fill you up. A typical glass of white wine (120ml) amounts to 77 calories and 80 calories for red wine that is roughly an equivalent of 10 minutes sweaty session on a crossbar trainer in the gym. So my advice is to consume in moderation.

This is a book about the Japanese way of food and about discovering the joy and pleasure of delicious and easy Japanese-inspired home cooking and eating. I am certain that *The Chopsticks Diet* will help you to feel and look fantastic.

Here are some suggestions for what to eat for your three meals a day through the seasons.

Spring meal plan
- Japanese rice porridge (p19)
- Asparagus & anchovy domburi (p31) or Omusubi (rice balls) (p67) or Tofu salad (p82)
- Clam chowder miso soup with crispy deep-fried tofu (p126) or Bamboo shoot sushi (p133)

Summer meal plan
- Steamed green tea & blueberry muffins (p22) or a smoothie (p26)
- Courgette & tomato domburi (p32) or Chilled soba noodles with gazpacho sauce (p52) or any salads and why not try Baked aubergines with grated daikon on green tea soba noodles (p49)
- Classic salmon sashimi with daikon salad (p86) or Beef carpaccio & aubergine with ginger dressing (p100) or Chilled misopacho (p110) with any salads

Summer picnic
- Tofu Spanish omelette (p25), Rolled sushi (p62) to impress your friends or Fresh spring rolls (p68) and don't forget to take some salads

Autumn meal plan
- Swirled egg brown rice porridge (p21) or Tofu Spanish omelette (p25)
- Chilli mushrooms & tofu domburi (p34) or Spiced lentils with prawns (p38) or try Nori & rocket soba in broth (p50) or Japanese mushrooms with soba noodles in green tea broth (p51)
- Japanese mushroom miso soup (p113) or Creamy roast pumpkin miso soup (p114) or Sea bream on rice (p147)

Winter meal plan
- Adzuki & rice porridge (p20)
- Warm lentils with tofu and spinach (p40) or Crispy duck with orange & watercress salad (p103)
- Okonomiyaki (p122) or Country-style kayu with chicken (p140) or Salmon hotpot (p 152)

Ingredients

People tell me that the greatest barrier to learning Japanese cooking is not so much the cooking techniques but the ingredients. Faced with un-familiar foods, even the most adventurous cook may be perplexed in a Japanese food store. The purpose of this section is to provide a simple and helpful guide to some Japanese ingredients that are used in this book. Included are notes about storage and how long foods will keep.

Azuki (Adzuki beans)

This small red bean is the second most frequently used legume in Japanese cooking, after the soy bean. Dried adzuki beans that need soaking and cooking are widely available in supermarkets and health shops. The ready-to-use tinned variety is also becoming easier to find in larger supermarkets. Store in a dry kitchen cupboard.

Daikon (Japanese giant white radish)

Daikon (pictured opposite top left) is aptly written as 'big root' in Japanese. A typical daikon grows about 35cm long, and as thick as a small marrow. Daikon is one of the most important ingredients in Japanese cooking and is easy to find in most Asian and Japanese stores outside Japan. Choose the one that feels solid, has tight skin and is free from bruises, and keep refrigerated. Daikon is also available in other forms. Pickled daikon – takuan – is bright yellow, crunchy and pungent. Dried and shredded daikon is called kiriboshi daikon and needs to be soaked before cooking.

Gobou (burdock)

This long, thin root vegetable has long been used by the Chinese in their herbal medicine; only the Japanese eat it. Covered in a dark brown skin, it can measure as much as 120cm in length but is usually about 45cm long. The skin has the most flavour, so it is best to scrub it clean. It must be submerged in cold water as soon as it is cut to stop discolouring and take away any bitterness. Fresh burdock is available all year round from Japanese food stores. Frozen pre-shaved burdock is also sold in bags in Japanese food stores.

Goma (sesame seeds)

Both white and black sesame seeds are used in Japanese cooking, either in whole or ground form. The taste and aroma of sesame seeds intensify when heated or ground. Ready-toasted sesame seeds are available from Japanese food stores. Store in lidded jars in a dry kitchen cupboard.

Hijiki (hijiki seaweed)

Hijiki is a twiggy, olive-brown marine plant that grows 30–100cm in height. In Japanese food stores or health shops outside Japan, it is nearly always sold in dried form. Dried hijiki must be soaked in water to reconstitute before use. It expands to nearly ten times its volume when softened. Store in a dark dry kitchen cupboard.

Kanten (agar agar)

Agar agar (pictured opposite top right) is a pure form of vegetarian gelatine, which is made of red seaweed, called tengusa (heavenly grass) in Japanese. It comes in three forms: bar, filament and powder. Outside Japan, you are most likely to find the powder form conveniently packed in 4g sachets that can be used like conventional gelatine powder. Compared to gelatine, agar agar sets more quickly, is more heat tolerant and, above all, is completely free of smell or taste and lacks the rubberiness of animal gelatine. Keep in a dark dry kitchen cupboard for up to 6 months.

Katsuo-bushi (bonito fish flakes)

The bonito, a member of the mackerel family, has been an important ingredient in Japanese cooking both as a

food and a seasoning ingredient. Fish flakes (pictured opposite top left) are made by shaving the dried and smoked fish fillet. The flakes look like pale rose-coloured wood shavings and have a distinct smoky aroma and taste. They are sold in cellophane packs of various sizes, from handy 4g single-use packets to more economical larger bags. If stored in a dark dry kitchen cupboard, flakes will keep for up to 12 months, but use within 3 months once the seal is opened.

Kome (rice)

Nearly half of the world's population depends on rice and in Japanese, the word *gohan* means both 'a meal' and 'cooked rice'. In other words, for the Japanese, a bowl of rice is a meal in itself; they are inseparable and it is almost impossible to talk about Japanese food without talking about rice. Highly polished white rice has always been at the top of the Japanese food hierarchy. The economic boom of the 1980s affected every aspect of life in Japan, including food, and the result was that the more exotic, expensive, and sometimes downright extravagant a food was, the more eagerly it was sought after. Even rice had to be a 'designer' or 'brand' food and became ever more processed. Fortunately, the excess did not last long and Japanese people returned to their previous way of eating, enjoying simple, frugal and more wholesome food. They didn't have to look very far but had only to embrace many of their traditional foods such as home-grown vegetables, seasonings such as miso and, above all, rice. The rice they now enjoyed was the rice once thought to be old-fashioned, unsophisticated, unpolished or half-polished: brown rice.

Brown rice is the most important source of energy in the Japanese diet. It is unmilled, leaving the bran, germ, and aleurone layers (just underneath the germ) intact. The nutrients occur mainly in the rice 'embryo', which is removed from processed rice when it is polished. Brown rice takes two to three times longer to cook and has a chewy texture. It is harder to digest and therefore sustains you for much longer. Brown rice also requires more chewing – a good habit to get into since it produces more saliva to aid digestion. The additional chewing slows down consumption.

There is a compromise called 'haiga seimai', which is a part-polished rice. The embryo is still intact and therefore contains about twice the amount of vitamins and minerals that white rice has. But it cooks more quickly than brown rice. Although all Japanese specialist grocers stock it, it is hard to distinguish from the ordinary, polished white rice since it is simply translated into English as 'rice'. My advice is to ask for help.

Konbu (kelp seaweed)

Konbu is one of the two basic ingredients for making dashi (Japanese stock), the stock on which numerous Japanese dishes depend on. There are many varieties and it is cultivated mainly in the cold waters off the northernmost island of Hokkaido. The typical deep olive brown kelp leaf grows 20cm wide and 10m long. Konbu is sold dried and cut into manageable lengths. Choose dark and thick ones and store in a dark dry kitchen cupboard for up to 12 months.

Konnyaku (devil's tongue)

Konnyaku (pictured opposite top right) must rank at the top of the list of Japan's strange foods. The root of this plant is made into a flour and compressed into a slab. Although there are many varieties of colour and shape, standard konnyaku sold in Japanese food stores in the West is grey with dark speckles, and it measures 15 x 7cm and 1.5cm thick. It is normally sold vacuum-packed with a little limewater. Store in a dark kitchen cupboard for up to 3 months but once opened, refrigerate in a clean bowl of water. Change the water daily and use within 2 weeks. All konnyaku should be boiled briefly before use.

Mirin (sweet cooking sake)

This sweetened cooking sake looks like a thin golden syrup and has a round, mild alcoholic aroma. It is used in cooking to add a sweet taste and to create a glossy appearance. Mirin is sold in bottles of various sizes. Store in a cool place, away from direct sunlight. Once the seal is broken, the aroma will begin to deteriorate and it should be kept refrigerated.

Miso (fermented soy bean paste)

Miso (pictured opposite bottom left) is one of the most important staples in Japanese cooking. There are numerous varieties, each with its own taste, aroma, colour and texture. The colour is generally a good guide to taste and texture – the lighter the colour, the less salty the flavour and the softer the texture. They are all made by essentially the same method: crushed, boiled soy beans, on their own or with rice, wheat or barley, are left to ferment and mature for months or even up to 3 years. In this book, I often recommend using more than one variety to create more interesting tastes so it might be helpful to buy small quantities of different types. Japanese food stores carry nearly a dozen different kinds of miso, and health shops often have at least half a dozen types. If refrigerated, miso will keep for up to 12 months in airtight containers.

Nori (laver seaweed)

Today nearly all nori is farmed. Spores are planted on nets placed in sheltered shallow bays in January and harvested in the autumn. Mature plants are gathered, washed in fresh water and laid in thin sheets to dry like handmade paper and then toasted. A sheet of dry, toasted nori comes in a standard size of 20 x 18cm and is sold in bundles of ten. The price is a good indication of the quality – choose thick, glossy, dark olive-brown sheets. Nori also comes ready-shredded or seasoned. It should be stored in a dark dry kitchen cupboard and once opened, nori should be kept in airtight plastic bags and used as soon as possible. If it becomes limp, toast it over a gentle flame to revive the aroma and crispness before use.

Rencon (lotus root)

Lotus root (pictured page 11 bottom left) is actually a buff-coloured rhizome, typically measuring nearly 1m long and 6cm thick. It is divided into cylinder-like segments, each up to 15cm. Air passages run through the length of the rhizome, which give it an attractive appearance in cross-section, like a paper-chain. Although fresh lotus roots are becoming more readily available from Asian and Japanese food stores, you are most likely to come across the 'fresh boiled' variety vacuum-packed with a little water or in cans. Fresh lotus roots should be stored in a cool dark place like potatoes, although they do not keep as long.

Sake

Sake, dashi, soy sauce, miso and rice vinegar are the 'big five' in Japanese cooking. In nearly every Japanese dish one or more of these ingredients is used. In cooking, sake is used to tenderise and to suppress saltiness; it also helps to eliminate fishy tastes and smells and to revive the delicate tastes of other ingredients. Although cheaper cooking sake is available, I do not recommend it, as it tends to have an inferior flavour and aroma. Besides, only a small amount is used in cooking. Sake is sold in bottles or cartons in various quantities in off licences, supermarkets or Japanese food stores. Once the seal is opened, keep it in a cool dark kitchen cupboard and use within 3 months.

Shoyu (soy sauce)

Soy sauce is one of the most important Japanese ingredients. It is made from fermented soy beans, water, salt and wheat. It has a beautiful spectrum of colours, ranging from warm amber and deep brown to shimmering purple. It also carries complex aromas. The fermentation of soy beans converts its protein into amino acids and the carbohydrate of the wheat into glucose that together give the distinct, appetising taste of soy sauce. Outside Japan, cooks are likely to find three types of soy sauce; an all-purpose dark soy; a saltier, light soy and the wheat-free and slightly thicker tamari. Buy small quantities, refrigerate after opening and use within a few months.

Soba (buckwheat noodle)

Soba noodles are made from buckwheat flour. Buckwheat is a fast growing, hardy annual plant native to central Asia and China. It has long been eaten in Japan, first as a cereal, in a dumpling form, and much later as noodles. It is difficult to make noodles with buckwheat flour exclusively as the buckwheat proteins are completely gluten-free and therefore do not bind easily into a noodle shape. So most soba noodles contain some wheat, mountain yam, or both, as binding agents. When cooking the soba noodles, a glass of cold water is poured into the saucepan of boiling water to bring down the temperature to ensure that the inner core of each noodle strand is cooked at the same rate as the outside.

Su (vinegar)

Japanese rice vinegar has a much milder strength than most western vinegars. The manufacturing process is a cross between that of sake and soy sauce. The rice is washed, soaked and steamed, and then yeast is added to form a rice culture that converts sake-like alcohol into vinegar. Most Japanese rice vinegars range in colour from pale golden to light bronze and have pleasant and mild yet astringent tastes and aromas. It is sold in bottles of different quantities in Japanese food stores and larger supermarkets. Store in a cool dark cupboard. Once opened, use within 6 months.

Takenoko (bamboo shoots)

Freshly dug bamboo shoots in their husks are the first sign of spring in Japan. In the West, bamboo shoots are available ready cooked in tins from Asian food stores or larger supermarkets. Freshly cooked shoots, vacuum-packed in water, are sold all year round in Japanese food stores. Wash thoroughly and remove the grainy white residue, a result of the commercial prepa-ration process, which has an unpleasant sour taste. Both tinned and water-packed bamboo shoots will keep for about a week if refrigerated in clean water. Change the water every day.

Tea

There are many varieties of green tea but for the purpose of this book, I use the ceremonial matcha/green tea powder and all-purpose sencha. Matcha is made from freshly picked young leaves that are steamed, dried and ground to a powder. It is expensive and sold in small quantities. Along with ordinary tea leaves, matcha and sencha should be stored in a dry cupboard away from direct sunlight.

Tofu

Tofu is soy bean curd made from coagulated soymilk. Soy beans are soaked overnight, boiled, ground and strained. A coagulant – magnesium chloride – is added to form a curd in a muslin-lined mould. Firm cotton tofu is slightly off-white and firm enough to handle, while soft silken tofu is pure white and more delicate. Fresh tofu is normally sold in a plastic container filled with a little water. Tofu is essentially a fresh food and should be used within a few days. Keep refrigerated in fresh water. Deep-fried tofu is often sold frozen. Once defrosted, it should be used within a few days.

Umeboshi (pickled plums)

Umeboshi (pictured page 12 bottom right) is made from unripe green plums, soaked in brine, packed with red perilla leaves, and left to pickle. It is sold in Japanese food stores or health shops in jars or plastic tabs. Once opened, it keeps almost indefinitely, if refrigerated.

Wakame (soft seaweed)

Wakame is a member of the brown algae family. In Japanese food stores, larger supermarkets and health shops outside Japan, wakame is nearly always sold in dried form. Before use, dried wakame must be soaked in water. Store in a dark dry kitchen cupboard.

Wasabi (Japanese green horseradish)

Wasabi (pictured page 11 bottom right) is written as 'mountain hollyhock' in Japanese and is one of the strongest spices used in Japanese cooking. Its natural habitat is the marshy edge of cold and clear mountain streams. Today nearly all fresh wasabi sold in Japan is cultivated in remote flooded mountain terraces. The root part of this perennial aquatic plant typically grows to the size of an average carrot but it is green and knobbly. Although many high-quality Japanese restaurants serve freshly grated wasabi, most Western home cooks are likely to encounter wasabi either in powder form or as a ready-mixed paste in a small plastic tube. Both powder and paste are sold in Japanese food stores or larger supermarkets. Treat the powder in the same way as English mustard powder and keep it in a dark dry kitchen cupboard. Wasabi paste needs to be refrigerated after opening and used within a few months.

Yuzu (Japanese citron)

The yuzu fruit is bright yellow and about the same size as a tangerine. It is used purely for its marvellous aromatic rind and fragrant juices. In the West, a fresh yuzu is difficult to find but the juice is sold in bottles in Japanese food stores. It is expensive but a little goes a long way. Keep refrigerated and shake well before use.

The traditional Japanese breakfast consists of a bowl of freshly cooked rice or rice porridge, a bowl of hot miso soup with tofu or wakame seaweed, a plate of grilled fish, simmered seasonal vegetables, an egg dish such as a rolled omelette, accompanied by side dishes such as a small helping of natto (sticky fermented soybeans), a tiny dish of seasoned seaweed or a few sheets of dried seasoned nori, and an assortment of pickled vegetables. It is a pretty long menu to prepare first thing in the morning and, to be honest, I doubt if many typical households in Japan today feature such an elaborate and labour-intensive fare every morning. Japanese people today reserve such a big breakfast tray for weekends or for when they are staying at an inn or a hotel on holiday. The everyday average Japanese breakfast is a much more simplified version of the menu above, although rice and miso soup always appear.

The Japanese love breakfast. The nation that has longer life spans than anyone else and enjoys a relatively good health knows the importance of a good breakfast. Do not skip breakfast — it is the most important meal of the day. Skipping breakfast will cause your blood-sugar level to drop so low that by mid-morning your brain is unable to concentrate, your tummy is rumbling, and you will be tempted to reach out for a quick sugar-fix such as a bar of chocolate. In an ideal world, I would feast like an emperor in the morning, eat like a queen at lunchtime and like a pauper in the evening. I think we all know the importance of breakfast and the harm caused by skipping it. But none of us lives in an ideal world and we all seem to be rushing out the door in the morning. This is why I have included a small number of delicious Japanese-inspired breakfast recipes that are 'doable' to get you started.

Breakfast

Japanese rice porridge

Serves 2

- 50g Japanese-style short grain rice
- 350ml water
- ¼ teaspoon salt
- a handful of raspberries

An eminent thirteenth-century Zen Buddhist monk, Dohgen, wrote that there are ten benefits to enjoy from a bowl of 'kayu', or Japanese rice porridge: it gives glossy and healthy skin, strengthens the body and soul, promotes longevity, is easy to digest and good for the brain, helps to maintain warmth, staves off hunger, quenches thirst and promotes healthy bowel movements. This all sounds excellent, if not almost too good to be true, considering it is only a humble bowl of soupy rice! There is a varying degree of consistency in Japanese rice porridge, depending on the amount of water. In this recipe, the rice is cooked with seven times the amount of water, which makes the porridge quite soupy and light but still sustaining. Try this with raspberries on top instead of the traditional accompaniment of umeboshi (pickled plums).

Put the rice in a sieve and wash it under cool, running water until the rinse water becomes clear. Ideally, washing the rice should be done at least half an hour before cooking to let the rice absorb the moisture and plump up. This can be done the night before.

However, if you forget and are short of time, put the washed rice in a saucepan with the measured amount of water and let it sit for 10 minutes before turning the heat on. The ideal saucepan is heavy-based with a tight-fitting lid. Put on the lid and bring the rice to boil over a high heat – this should take about 5 minutes. Move the lid slightly and reduce the heat to low to allow to simmer for 20–25 minutes.

Turn off the heat, season with the salt, replace the lid and let it steam for 5 minutes. Garnish with raspberries and serve in small, warmed bowls with chopsticks.

Adzuki and rice porridge

Serves 2

- 25g dried adzuki beans, soaked in water overnight
- 600ml water
- 50g Japanese-style short grain rice, washed and then drained for 30 minutes

Adzuki beans have long been associated with auspiciousness in Japan. According to custom, adzuki porridge is eaten on the 15th January to celebrate the Little New Year on the old lunar calendar. Indeed, no celebration feast is complete without adzuki rice. The main components of adzuki beans are glucose and protein but their rich vitamin B1, potassium and highly edible fibre help to lower blood pressure, overcome fatigue and reduce swellings. Together, its gentle, sweet taste and warm pink appearance make this porridge a cheerful breakfast.

Put the adzuki beans in a heavy-based saucepan (do not use a cast iron saucepan as the iron reacts and will discolour the beans). Add the measured amount of water and cook over a medium heat until the beans become tender – this should take about 30–40 minutes. Top up with boiling water if necessary. Save the cooking juice and measure it to 500ml.

Put the rice and adzuki cooking juice in a heavy-based saucepan with a lid and bring to the boil over a high heat. Move the lid to prevent it from boiling over. Reduce the heat to low to simmer for a further 20 minutes. Turn off the heat, replace the lid and steam for 5 minutes. Serve hot in warmed bowls with chopsticks.

Tip
Because adzuki beans require long and slow cooking, I recommend cooking a large quantity and then keeping it refrigerated in the cooking juice for up to a week.

Swirled egg brown rice porridge

Serves 2

- 50g brown rice, soaked in water overnight
- 600ml water
- 2 eggs, lightly beaten
- 1 tablespoon soy sauce
- 2 spring onions, finely chopped
- a handful of shredded nori

Brown rice is much healthier than polished white rice and should become a staple in your diet. It needs one third more water to cook than polished white rice and takes a little longer to cook. It also requires much more chewing to get the full benefits and this is good news, especially for slimmers, because brown rice will keep you feeling satisfied much longer.

Start by soaking the rice with the measured amount of water in a heavy-based saucepan overnight. Place a tight-fitting lid on the saucepan and bring to the boil over a medium heat, then reduce the heat slightly and continue to cook for a further 40–45 minutes.

Add the beaten eggs, stir to swirl and season with the soy sauce. Garnish with spring onions and nori and serve with chopsticks.

Tip
Cooking with a pressure cooker will halve the preparation time.

Steamed green tea and blueberry muffins

Makes 6 regular muffins

- 75g caster sugar
- 75ml water
- 1 egg, lightly beaten
- 1 tablespoon vegetable oil
- 200g wholemeal flour
- 2 teaspoons baking powder
- 1 teaspoon matcha (green tea powder), plus extra for garnish
- 50g fresh blueberries

This recipe is so simple that you can easily make these delicious muffins for breakfast. If well wrapped, the muffins will keep for 3 days so they are brilliant for breakfast on the run.

Put the sugar and water in a saucepan and bring to the boil while stirring to dissolve all the sugar. Leave aside to cool.

Put the egg in a bowl, add the sugar water and whisk to mix well. Gradually add the oil into the mixture and sift in the flour, baking powder and the tea and fold in the blueberries.

Spoon the mixture into muffin cases or a lightly greased muffin tin. Place the tin in a rapidly boiling steamer and steam for 15 minutes. (If the muffin tin doesn't fit place the muffins into muffin cases and steam in batches.) Sprinkle with a little macha to serve.

Tofu Spanish omelette

Serves 2

- 100g soft silken tofu
- 1 teaspoon vegetable oil
- 3 eggs, lightly beaten
- 1 tablespoon light soy sauce
- 1 medium tomato, deseeded and roughly chopped
- 2 spring onions, roughly chopped

This adaptation of the rustic Spanish recipe uses tofu instead of potatoes which makes it a real 'power breakfast' that is easy to digest.

Drain the tofu by wrapping it in a piece of kitchen paper and microwaving it for 1 minute on medium. Cut into 2cm cubes.

Heat the oil in a small omelette pan over a medium heat. Mix the eggs and the soy sauce and add to the pan to cook for 2–3 minutes or until the outer edge becomes set but still runny in the centre.

Add the tofu, tomato and spring onions to cook for a further 2 minutes. To turn over the omelette, take the pan off the heat, slide the omelette on to a dinner plate, cover the omelette with the pan and turn over both the plate and the pan.

Return the pan to the heat to cook for 3–4 minutes or until the underside is cooked. Transfer the omelette to a chopping board, cut it into bite-size wedges and serve.

Japanese rolled omelette with nori

Serves 2

- 3 eggs
- 1 tablespoon mirin
- 2 teaspoons light soy sauce
- 1/2 teaspoon vegetable oil
- 2 sheets of nori, torn into small pieces

You need a small non-stick omelette pan for this recipe.

Put the eggs, mirin and soy sauce in a small bowl and beat lightly to mix. Heat the omelette pan over a medium heat and brush with the oil. Pour over a third of the egg mixture and when the surface begins to dry, add a third of the torn nori pieces to roughly cover the egg.

Gather the omelette towards you and pour in another third of the egg mixture. Repeat the cooking process until you have used all the egg mixture and the nori.

Transfer the omelette on to a chopping board, roll tightly and cut into bite-size pieces and serve with chopsticks.

Smoothies

Serves 2

Pictured are:
Green Tea and Tofu Smoothie and
Tofu and Stawberry Smoothie

Tofu and apple smoothie

- 100g soft silken tofu
- 2 apples, peeled, cored and roughly chopped
- 200ml apple juice
- 2 tablespoons runny honey
- 2.5cm fresh root ginger, peeled and roughly chopped

Put all the ingredients in a blender or food processor, and blend until smooth.

Tofu and strawberry smoothie

- 100g soft silken tofu
- 100g strawberries, stems removed
- 200ml soy milk
- 2 tablespoons runny honey

Put all the ingredients in a blender or food processor, and blend until smooth and serve.

Green tea and tofu smoothie

- 100g soft silken tofu
- 200ml soy milk
- 1 teaspoon matcha (green tea powder)
- 1 tablespoon kinako (soy bean flour)
- 2 tablespoons soft dark brown sugar

Put all the ingredients in a blender or food processor, and blend until smooth.

Green tea milkshake

- 2 bananas, roughly chopped
- 1 kiwi fruit, roughly chopped
- 200ml soy milk
- 1 teaspoon matcha (green tea powder)
- 2 tablespoons runny honey

Put all the ingredients in a blender or food processor, and blend until smooth.

Lunch in the Japanese culinary history became established sometime around the seventeenth century when food productions, and especially rice increased. After breakfast, lunch is the second most important meal of the day, especially for those watching their weight as there are still many hours left to burn off the food before bedtime. Based on their health benefits, I have selected two good carbohydrates, which are major sources of energy – rice and soba noodles – and designed the recipes around them. They are delicious, easy-to-prepare and guaranteed to leave you feeling satisfied, without feeling bloated or sleepy (like some processed carbohydrates can), for many guilt-free hours afterwards.

Rice and soba noodles can be eaten either hot or cold and lend themselves to microwave reheating if preferred, especially if you are taking them to work to eat for lunch (always make sure your rice is piping hot). Soba noodles are made of buckwheat flour that is completely gluten-free, rich in edible fibre and contains vitamin P that not only helps to lower cholesterol and is an antioxidant, but recent researches show it helps to prevent accumulation of body fat.

Domburi is the generic term for all-in-one-bowl rice food, typically served to busy people at lunch times. Traditional toppings such as chicken and egg, or sautéed beef and onion are served on top of rice in a ceramic bowl with a lid. I have applied the basic concept of domburi to create delicious and healthy one-course lunches. The domburi is also versatile and practical – leftovers from previous evening meals are easily adaptable to make domburi toppings. So there is no excuse for an unhealthy lunch!

One-bowl lunches

How to cook brown rice

Brown rice is 74–77 per cent carbohydrate and 6 per cent protein (the remaining 20 per cent is water, fibre, oil, vitamins and minerals). It is the single most important source of energy in the Japanese diet. Compared to white rice, it contains four times the amount of edible fibre, vitamins B1 and E, twice the amount of vitamin B2, minerals and oil. Brown rice needs a brief rinse under cold, running water, removing anything that floats to the surface. Leave the rinsed rice in a bowl of clean water for at least 2–3 hours, but ideally overnight. The amount of water needed to cook the rice depends on how long the rice has been soaked; the shorter the soaking time, the more water is required. If the rice has been left to soak overnight, add 20 per cent more water than the weight of rice. In other words, if you have 100g rice, add 120ml water. Use as solid and heavy-based a saucepan as possible, with a sturdy lid. Put the rice and water in the pan with the lid on and bring to the boil over a very gentle heat. Turn up the heat to medium when steam starts to escape and cook until the steam begins to slow down. Turn off the heat, but do not remove the lid. Leave to cook in the retained heat for a further 10–15 minutes before fluffing the rice.

Asparagus & anchovy domburi

Asparagus is a highly seasonal vegetable, so I try to eat as much of it as possible when it is available. In this quick-and-easy recipe, all the asparagus flavour is captured in the sauce.

Heat the oil in a frying pan over a medium heat and sauté the anchovies first, then add the garlic and asparagus. Lower the heat slightly and add the water and the onion soy-dashi sauce to season. When the cooking juice starts to boil, add the diluted agar agar to thicken the sauce.

Put the rice in warmed bowls, top with the asparagus mixture and sprinkle over the sesame seeds. Serve with chopsticks.

Serves 2

- 1 tablespoon vegetable oil
- 2 anchovy fillets, chopped
- 1 teaspoon garlic, finely minced
- 6 asparagus spears, cut diagonally into bite-size pieces
- 2 tablespoons water
- 2 tablespoons Onion Soy-Dashi Sauce (page 40)
- 1/4 teaspoon agar agar, diluted in 1 teaspoon water
- 200g warm, cooked rice (see above)
- 1 teaspoon toasted sesame seeds

Courgette & tomato domburi

This is a fast summer dish with a Japanese twist. Be sure to get very fresh and plump courgettes.

Put the oil in a pan over a medium heat and sauté the courgettes for 1 minute. Add the anchovies and garlic, shaking the pan a few times.

Reduce the heat slightly and add the tomato juice, sake and soy sauce to season. Let the cooking juice come to the boil, turn off the heat and stir in the miso paste.

Divide the rice between two warmed bowls, top with the courgette mixture, garnish with the chopped parsley and serve with chopsticks.

Serves 2

- 1 tablespoon olive oil
- 2 medium courgettes, peeled and diced
- 2 anchovy fillets, roughly chopped
- 1 garlic clove, finely minced
- 4 tablespoons tomato juice
- 2 tablespoons sake
- 2 teaspoons soy sauce
- 1 tablespoon miso paste
- 200g warm, cooked rice (page 31)
- a few sprigs of flat-leaf parsley, finely chopped

Egg & spinach domburi

Egg is a classic ingredient for domburi topping since it is quick and versatile. To achieve the correct consistency for domburi toppings the eggs should be cooked until just before they set, so that the egg binds the other ingredients together while still retaining enough moisture to act as a sauce over the rice.

Cut the leek lengthways and finely slice diagonally. Place the leek and the water in a saucepan and bring to the boil over a low to medium heat.

Lower the heat slightly and add the spinach, sake, mirin, sugar and soy sauce. Gently pour in the beaten eggs and stir. Turn off the heat when the egg mixture just starts to set and serve over the rice. Garnish with the shredded nori and serve immediately.

Tip
Try not to over-cook. It is better to stop cooking earlier rather than later as the retained heat will continue to cook the eggs.

Serves 2

- ½ leek, trimmed
- 100ml water
- 50g baby spinach leaves
- 2 tablespoons sake
- 2 tablespoons mirin
- ½ tablespoon sugar
- 3 tablespoons soy sauce
- 2 eggs, lightly beaten
- 200g warm, cooked rice (page 31)
- a small handful of shredded nori

Chilli mushrooms & tofu domburi

This is a gutsy, wholesome vegetarian dish that is sure to leave you feeling very satisfied. Adjust the amount of chilli to suit your heat tolerance.

Serves 2

- 200g firm cotton tofu
- 6 medium chestnut mushrooms
- 4 shiitake mushrooms
- 1/2 packet shimeji mushrooms
- 1/2 tablespoon vegetable oil
- 1/2 onion, finely minced
- 2 teaspoons fresh root ginger, grated or finely minced
- 1 garlic clove, finely minced
- 1/4–1/2 large red chilli, deseeded and finely chopped
- 2 tablespoons sake
- 1 tablespoon soy sauce
- 1 tablespoon medium-coloured or red miso
- 1 teaspoon chilli sauce (optional)
- 200g warm, cooked rice (page 31)

Start by dicing the tofu into 1cm cubes. Blanch the cubes in boiling water and drain.

Chop the chestnut mushrooms into four wedges. Cut the shiitake mushrooms into wedges the same size as the chestnut mushrooms, discarding the stems. Cut off the jointed base of the shimeji mushrooms and separate. (If you can't find this mushroon variety, use more of the others.)

Heat the oil in a pan over a low heat and sweat the onion until soft. Add the tofu, ginger, garlic, chilli and the mushrooms and cook for 2–3 minutes. Add the sake and soy sauce to season and let the cooking juice start to bubble.

Turn off the heat and stir in the miso paste. Taste and adjust the seasoning. If you like more heat, add the chilli sauce. Divide the rice between two bowls, spoon the mushroom mix over the rice and serve with chopsticks.

Seafood & wild rocket domburi

This is a fusion-flavoured domburi dish – part Italian and Thai – very quick and easy to make.

Make shallow incisions over the body of the squid and cut into bite-size pieces. Chop the tentacles into pieces of a manageable length. Put both the squid and the prawns in a bowl, sprinkle over the cornflour and salt.

Heat the olive oil in a pan over a gentle heat and infuse the garlic. Add the prawns and squid and sauté until opaque. Season with the chilli and nam pla. Turn off the heat and quickly stir in the rocket leaves to wilt in the residual heat.

Put the rice into two warmed bowls and top with the seafood mixture. Serve with chopsticks.

Serves 2

- 100g small squid, cleaned
- 100g peeled, uncooked prawns
- 2 teaspoons cornflour
- $^1/_2$ teaspoon salt
- 2 tablespoons olive oil
- 1 garlic clove, finely minced
- pinch of chilli flakes
- 2 teaspoons nam pla (Thai fish sauce)
- 25g wild rocket leaves, washed, drained and roughly chopped
- 200g warm, cooked rice (page 31)

Broad bean & crabmeat domburi

The sweetness of the broad beans and the white crabmeat are perfectly matched in this recipe.

Start by cooking the broad beans for 2–3 minutes. Drain, rinse in cold water and then remove their outer skin (I am sorry, this is rather fiddly but the result is well worth the extra effort!).

Place the broad beans and crabmeat in a saucepan with the sake and bring to the boil over a medium heat. Season with salt and freshly ground white pepper to taste. Add the diluted agar agar to the sauce and let it come to the boil for a minute or two to thicken the cooking juice.

Put the rice into two warmed bowls, top with the broad bean mixture and garnish with the grated zest. Serve with chopsticks.

Serves 2

- 100g broad beans (shelled weight)
- 75g white crabmeat
- 4 tablespoons sake
- $^1/_4$ teaspoon agar agar, diluted in 1 teaspoon water
- 200g warm, cooked rice (page 31)
- 1 teaspoon lemon or lime zest, finely grated
- salt and freshly ground white pepper

Spiced lentils with prawns

Serves 2

- 200g Puy lentils
- 100g frozen sweetcorn
- 2 spring onions, finely chopped
- 2 medium vine tomatoes, deseeded and roughly chopped
- 1/2 green chilli pepper, deseeded and finely chopped
- a handful of fresh coriander, finely chopped
- 2 tablespoons soy sauce
- 2 tablespoons extra-virgin olive oil
- 200g cooked ready-to-eat prawns
- salt and freshly ground black pepper

This is a wonderful combination of flavours and because it's so easy to make, it's a great lunch dish for busy people who need to eat well.

Put the lentils in a saucepan, cover with water and cook over a medium heat for 20–25 minutes, or until the lentils are soft but not mushy. Drain, rinse under cold running water and drain well. Cook the frozen sweetcorn for 3–5 minutes and drain.

In a bowl, mix together the lentils, sweetcorn, spring onions, tomatoes, chilli and coriander. Add the soy sauce, olive oil and adjust the seasoning to taste with salt and freshly ground black pepper.

Divide the lentil mixture between two serving plates, arrange the prawns on top and serve with chopsticks.

Tuna, tomato & okra domburi

Serves 2

- 6 okra
- salt and and freshly ground black pepper
- 2 ripe vine-tomatoes, skinned and roughly chopped
- 50g tinned tuna, drained
- 2 tablespoons Onion Soy-Dashi Sauce (page 40)
- 200g warm cooked rice (page 31)
- a few basil leaves, finely torn

I have used tinned tuna here for ease, but of course if you have a delicious tuna steak in the fridge, treat yourself for lunch!

Sprinkle a pinch of salt on the okra and rub them gently together to remove the very fine hairs. Blanch the okra quickly, discarding the tops, then slice into 5mm pieces. Place the okra slices in a bowl. Season with salt and freshly ground black pepper. Stir to develop the characteristic stickiness.

Add the tomatoes, tuna and 2 tablespoons of onion soy-dashi sauce. Stir to combine the mixture.

Put the warm rice into two bowls, top with the tomato and okra mixture and garnish with basil. Serve with chopsticks.

Warm lentils with tofu and spinach

Serves 2

For the onion soy-dashi sauce
- 200ml soy sauce
- 200ml mirin
- 1/2 onion, grated
- 1 garlic clove, grated
- 5cm square piece of konbu

- 200g Puy lentils
- 2 garlic cloves, slightly crushed with the side of a knife
- 1 red pepper
- 1 yellow pepper
- 100g firm cotton tofu
- 100g baby spinach leaves, washed and drained
- 2 tablespoons Onion Soy-Dashi Sauce
- 1 tablespoon good-quality balsamic vinegar
- 1 tablespoon extra-virgin olive oil

The slightly peppery-tasting Puy lentils and gentle tofu are a perfect match in this sustaining lunch dish.

To make the onion soy-dashi sauce, place all the ingredients for the sauce in a saucepan and bring to the boil over a low heat. Reduce the heat and simmer for 8–10 minutes. Turn off the heat and let the sauce cool before straining it through a fine mesh sieve. The sauce will keep for two weeks refrigerated in a glass bottle. This is a tasty, versatile sauce and will feature in many recipes.

Put the lentils in a saucepan, cover with water, add the garlic and bring to the boil. Reduce the heat and simmer for 20–25 minutes, or until the lentils are soft but not mushy. Remove the garlic, drain and set the lentils aside to keep warm.

Place the peppers under a preheated grill, turning occasionally until the skins blacken. When the skins are completely black, put the peppers inside a resealable plastic bag to sweat, then remove the skins and discard the seeds. Reserve the juices and slice the flesh into thin strips.

While the peppers are grilling, wrap the tofu in sheets of kitchen paper and leave it to drain on a slightly tilted chopping board for 20 minutes and place a plate with a little weight on top of the tofu to speed up the draining. Or, if you are really pressed, microwave on medium for 1 minute.

Put the spinach, lentils, peppers with the juices, and tofu in a mixing bowl. Pour over the onion soy-dashi sauce, balsamic vinegar and olive oil. Gently stir to mix and serve with chopsticks.

Stir-fry soy beans with spicy miso

Serves 2

- 100g dried soy beans, soaked overnight (see Tip)
- ½ tablespoon vegetable oil
- 50g minced pork
- 1 onion, peeled and finely minced
- 1 carrot, peeled and finely chopped
- 1 garlic clove, crushed and finely minced
- 1 tablespoon sake
- 1 tablespoon soy sauce
- 1 tablespoon chilli sauce
- 2 tablespoons medium-coloured miso paste
- 200g warm, cooked rice (page 31)
- 1 spring onion, finely chopped diagonally
- a small handful of watercress

You need to soak the beans overnight then simmer for about an hour. I am afraid it is a rather lengthy process so I recommend cooking a large quantity and freezing what you don't use. Or, if you are in hurry, use tinned soy beans, which are now widely available.

Drain the soy beans, place in a pan covered with fresh water and cook over a moderate heat for 45–60 minutes. Reserve 50ml of the cooking water. If you are using tinned soy beans, add 50ml water instead.

Heat a wok over a medium heat, add the oil and stir-fry the pork for 3 minutes. Add the onion and carrot and cook for 2 minutes before adding the garlic to cook for a further 3 minutes.

Reduce the heat slightly and add the soy beans, reserved cooking water, sake and soy sauce. Continue to cook while stirring constantly until the cooking juice has almost evaporated. Turn off the heat, stir in the chilli sauce and miso paste. Mix well to incorporate.

Divide the rice between two bowls, top with the bean mixture and garnish with the spring onion and watercress. Serve with chopsticks.

Tip
If you are using a tinned variety of soy beans, allow 200g.

Soba noodles with Chinese cabbage & tofu

Serves 2

- 1 postcard-size piece of konbu
- 200g dried soba noodles
- 2 tablespoons olive oil
- 100g Chinese cabbage, finely chopped
- $1/2$ teaspoon salt
- 1 tablespoon white, toasted sesame seeds, finely ground
- 100g soft silken tofu, diced
- 1 tablespoon soy milk
- 1 tablespoon white miso
- 1 teaspoon toasted sesame seeds

Try to use soba noodles when making these recipes. Soba is rich in edible fibre which helps to lower cholesterol, but the most noteworthy nutrient is rutin (a kind of vitamin P), which strengthens capillary vessels and helps to prevent high blood pressure and brain haemorrhages. It is also an antioxidant. But wait for it... recent research shows that soba proteins prevent the accumulation of body fats – perfect for a slimming diet. This is a gentle, beautifully creamy noodle sauce made with tofu, sesame seeds and white miso. In spite of appearing mild, it is packed with flavour and high-quality vegetable proteins.

Put the konbu in a saucepan of cold water and bring to a simmer over a low heat. Take out the konbu when it floats to the surface and the water begins to boil. Take out a ladleful of water and reserve it for later. Let the water come back to a rolling boil.

Add the noodles and stir to separate them. Pour in a glass of cold water when the water begins to rise to the top of the saucepan. The noodles are ready when the water comes back to the boil. Drain, rinse under cold running water and set aside to drain well.

Put the olive oil in a frying pan and cook the Chinese cabbage over a moderate heat. Sprinkle in the salt to encourage the cabbage to soften. When the cabbage is soft, add the reserved konbu water, ground sesame, tofu and soy milk. Simmer and reduce for 5–8 minutes.

Add the miso and stir well to mix. Put the soba noodles in the sauce and stir to combine.

Turn off the heat, divide the noodles on to two serving plates, sprinkle with the sesame seeds and serve with chopsticks.

Wakame & spinach soba noodles with sesame dipping sauce

Spinach is a super health food – it is packed with vitamins B and C, anti-cancerous beta carotene and various minerals, especially iron. In this recipe you get the double benefits of both wakame and spinach.

Put the wakame in a bowl of water at room temperature to soften for 5 minutes and then drain.

Serves 2

- 40g dried wakame
- 200g dried soba noodles
- 200g spinach, cut into stems and leaves, washed and drained
- 1 spring onion, finely chopped diagonally
- 2 tablespoons shredded nori
- Japanese seven spice chilli pepper or chilli pepper (optional)

For the sesame dipping sauce

- 4 tablespoons toasted sesame seeds
- 4 tablespoons Onion Soy-Dashi Sauce (page 40)
- 125ml water

To prepare the dipping sauce, put the sesame seeds in a mortar and grind them to a coarse powder. Add the onion soy-dashi sauce and dilute with the water. Divide the sauce mixture into two cups and set aside.

Meanwhile bring a large saucepan of water to the boil over a high heat and add the soba noodles. Stir to separate the noodles. Adjust the heat if necessary to prevent the water from boiling over and cook the noodles for 2–3 minutes. Add the spinach, root and stem parts first, adding the soft leaves and wakame later.

Just as the water comes back to the boil and begins to rise, turn off the heat and quickly drain into a sieve. Run the sieve under cold, running water to refresh the noodles and the vegetables.

Drain well and divide on to two serving plates. Garnish with the chopped spring onion, shredded nori and chilli pepper, if using. Serve with the dipping sauce and chopsticks.

Soba noodles with umeboshi & sprouting broccoli

Serves 2

- 200g dried soba noodles
- 2 tablespoons extra-virgin olive oil
- 2 garlic cloves, thinly sliced
- 1/4 teaspoon salt
- 100g sprouting broccoli, cut into bite-size pieces
- 2 umeboshi, stones removed and chopped
- 1/2 tablespoon toasted sesame seeds

Pickled plums are called umeboshi in Japanese and are a staple in Japanese kitchen cupboards because they are believed to be an edible cure-all.

Bring a large saucepan of water to the boil, add the noodles and stir to separate them. At the same time, heat the oil, garlic and salt in a generous-sized frying pan over a low heat to infuse the oil with a garlic flavour.

When the saucepan of water comes back to the boil, add the broccoli to cook for 1 minute. Pour in a glass of cold water when the water starts to rise to the top. Let the water return to the boil for the third time, then turn off the heat. Drain and rinse under cold, running water. Drain well again. Take the garlic out of the frying pan and add the noodle mixture to briefly sauté.

Turn off the heat, add the umeboshi and stir together. Divide the noodle mixture into two equal portions, sprinkle the sesame seeds to garnish and serve with chopsticks.

Baked aubergines with grated daikon on green tea soba noodles

Serves 2

- 1 aubergine, pricked
- 200g dried green tea soba noodles
- 200g daikon, scrubbed clean
- 4 tablespoons Onion Soy-Dashi Sauce (page 40)
- 2 teaspoons grated fresh root ginger

This is another recipe with the wonderfully refreshing grated daikon that counterbalances the rich taste of aubergines. Try and use green tea-infused soba noodles so you gain all the nutritional benefits of eating green tea as well as the goodness of the noodles.

Place the aubergine to blacken all over under a grill preheated to its highest setting. When the aubergine is cool enough to handle, peel the skin by running a bamboo skewer just beneath the skin. Cut the flesh into strips and set aside.

Bring a saucepan of water to the boil, add the noodles and stir to separate the strands. When the water comes back to the boil and begins to rise to the top, pour in a glass of cold water. Let the water return to the boil for a third time, drain, rinse under cold running water and drain again.

Meanwhile, grate the daikon and squeeze gently in your hand, fluff up the pulp, and reserve the juice to mix with the onion soy-dashi sauce. Mix the grated ginger with the onion soy-dashi sauce.

Divide the noodles into two equal portions on serving dishes and pour over the onion soy-dashi sauce. Put the grated daikon over the noodles and top with the aubergine strips. Serve with chopsticks.

Nori & rocket soba in broth

This is an updated version of a classic soba noodle dish called hanamaki soba, which is a simple soba in broth with crushed nori. This noodle sauce can accompany many noodle dishes – use it as a base to create your own healthy variations.

Serves 2

For the noodle sauce
- 1 postcard-size piece of konbu
- 200ml soy sauce
- 4 tablespoons sugar
- 2 tablespoons mirin

- 200g dried soba noodles
- 100g rocket leaves
- 1 postcard-size piece of konbu
- 300ml water
- 2 sheets nori
- 2 spring onions, finely chopped
- ½ teaspoon chilli pepper

Start preparing the noodle sauce by placing the konbu in a saucepan with all the other ingredients and set aside for at least 30 minutes, but ideally 1 hour, before heating it over a low heat.

Take the konbu out and simmer for 5–7 minutes before turning off the heat. Let it cool to room temperature and refrigerate in a sterilised glass jar with a lid. The sauce will keep for 4 weeks in the fridge. The sauce is used as a base for noodle broth, or as a noodle-dipping sauce.

Bring a saucepan of water to the boil, add the noodles and stir to separate the strands. When the water comes back to the boil and begins to rise to the top, pour in a glass of cold water. Let the water return to the boil for a third time, drain, rinse under cold running water and drain again. Divide the noodles into two bowls with the rocket leaves.

Meanwhile, put the konbu in a saucepan with the 300ml water and bring up to a simmer over a low heat. Take the konbu out just before the water reaches the boil, add 4 tablespoons of the noodle sauce and let it come up to the boil. Turn off the heat and ladle the broth over the noodles.

Crush the nori with your hands over the bowls of noodles, garnish with the spring onions, sprinkle over the chilli pepper and serve immediately with chopsticks.

Japanese mushrooms with soba noodles in green tea broth

Mushrooms are low in calories, contain no fat, are rich in edible fibre, vitamins B and D and are packed with flavours. These mysterious fungi are a tasty ally for dieters. In this recipe, I combine the smoky flavour of Japanese mushrooms with refreshing green tea to make a wonderful noodle broth.

Start by preparing the green tea mix by finely grinding the sesame seeds with a pestle and mortar. Add the remaining ingredients and grind the mixture further to incorporate completely.

Slice the shiitake mushrooms, discarding the stems. Cut off the bases of both the shimeji and enoki mushrooms where they join, and separate them. Strip the oyster mushrooms by hand.

Mix the water with the noodle sauce in a saucepan, add the mushrooms and cook over a medium heat. Lower the heat so the broth doesn't boil. Add the green tea mix and the agar agar to thicken.

Meanwhile, bring a saucepan of water to the boil, add the noodles and stir to separate the strands. When the water comes back to the boil and begins to rise to the top, pour in a glass of cold water. Let the water return to the boil for a third time, drain, rinse under cold running water and drain again.

Divide the noodles into two warmed bowls, pour over the broth, garnish with the spring onions and serve with chopsticks.

Tip
The green tea mix will keep for up to 4 weeks in an airtight container placed in the fridge. It makes a wonderful hot drink substitute for coffee.

Serves 2

For the green tea mix
- 2 tablespoons toasted black sesame seeds, finely ground
- 1 tablespoon match (green tea powder)
- 2 tablespoons kinako (soy bean flour)
- 3 tablespoons dark brown sugar

- 4 fresh shiitake mushrooms
- 1 pack of shimeji mushrooms
- 1 pack of enoki mushrooms
- 6 medium oyster mushrooms
- 300ml water
- 4 tablespoons Noodle Sauce (opposite page)
- 2 teaspoons green tea mix (see above)
- $1/4$ teaspoon agar agar, diluted in 1 teaspoon of water
- 200g dried soba noodles
- 2 spring onions, finely chopped

Chilled soba noodles with gazpacho sauce

Serves 2

- 200g dried soba noodles
- 1 tablespoon extra-virgin olive oil
- a few sprigs of flat parsley

For the gazpacho sauce
- 100ml tomato juice
- $1/2$ white or red onion, finely chopped
- $1/2$ red pepper, finely chopped
- $1/2$ yellow pepper, finely chopped
- 1 celery stick, finely chopped
- $1/2$ baby cucumber
- salt and freshly ground black pepper

This is a vibrant, fresh tomato-based pasta sauce that goes perfectly with Japanese soba noodles. Trust me, you will love it.

Bring a saucepan of water to the boil, add the noodles and stir to separate the strands. When the water comes back to the boil and begins to rise to the top, pour in a glass of cold water. Let the water return to the boil for a third time, drain, rinse under cold running water, coat the noodles with the oil to stop them from sticking together, and refrigerate in a colander over a bowl to drain further while you make the sauce.

Put all the ingredients for the sauce in a big bowl and stir to combine. Take out a couple of tablespoons of the sauce and set aside. Add the noodles to the bowl and mix.

Arrange the noodle mixture on two serving plates, top with `the reserved sauce, garnish with the chopped parsley and serve with chopsticks.

Seared scallops & soba noodles with mizuna pesto

Serves 2

For the mizuna pesto
- 100g mizuna leaves, washed and roughly chopped
- 2 tablespoons pine nuts
- 1 garlic clove, crushed
- 1/2 teaspoon wasabi paste
- 1/2 teaspoon salt
- 4 tablespoons extra-virgin olive oil, plus extra for drizzling

- 2 teaspoons vegetable oil
- 4 large, fresh, hand-dived scallops
- 200g dried soba noodles
- 50g wild rocket leaves
- 1 spring onion, finely chopped

Mizuna is a highly-decorative, green, leafy vegetable that originates in both China and Japan. It grows in a bushy clump of big green rosettes; the upper part resembles serrated wild rocket leaves, while the lower part of each leaf is a slender and firm white stalk. Mizuna also tastes similar to peppery wild rocket but has a juicier crunchy texture. Nutritionally, mizuna is about 95 per cent water and contains high levels of vitamins A and C, which are both good for the skin. It also contains various minerals, including calcium and iron.

It is getting easier to find in Asian grocers, especially in the winter and autumn, but a mixture of rocket and spinach makes a good substitute for this recipe.

Make the mizuna pesto by putting all the ingredients for the pesto in a food processor and blending until smooth. It will make about 150ml. Transfer to a plastic container, drizzle over some olive oil to cover the top surface, replace the lid and refrigerate to keep for up to 1 week.

Preheat a cast-iron griddle over a medium heat. Slice the scallops in half, coat with the vegetable oil and griddle for 20–30 seconds on each side. Transfer to a plate to keep warm.

Meanwhile, bring a saucepan of water to the boil, add the soba noodles and stir to ensure that the noodle strands are separated. When the water returns to the boil and begins to rise to the top, add a glass of cold water and let it return to the boil for the third time. Drain and rinse under hot running water and drain well again. Put the noodles back into the same saucepan (which should be still warm), add the rocket leaves and 1 1/2 tablespoons of pesto and stir to mix evenly.

Divide the noodles between two serving plates, arrange the scallops on the top and garnish with the spring onion. Serve with chopsticks.

Swirling egg soba noodles in broth

Serves 2

- 300ml water
- 4 tablespoons Noodle Sauce (page 50)
- ½ teaspoon agar agar, diluted in 2 teaspoons water
- 200g dried soba noodles
- 1 egg, lightly beaten
- 1 sheet nori, crushed into small pieces
- 1 tablespoon cress
- 2 teaspoons grated fresh root ginger

This pretty noodle dish is very quick to make and so it's useful as a recipe to have up your sleeve when you want an instant, healthy lunch.

Mix the water with the noodle sauce in a saucepan. Bring to just below the boil over a medium heat, add the agar agar to thicken and lower the heat to simmering point.

Bring another saucepan of water to the boil, add the noodles and stir to separate the strands. When the water comes back to the boil and begins to rise to the top, pour in a glass of cold water. Let the water return to the boil for a third time, drain, rinse under cold running water and drain again.

Pour the beaten egg into the broth. Wait for a moment and then stir with a pair of chopsticks, swirling the egg. Turn off the heat.

Divide the noodles into two warm bowls and ladle over the broth. Garnish with the crushed nori, cress and small mounds of grated ginger. Serve immediately with chopsticks.

Sobaghetti with broccoli & tofu

Serves 2

- 100g firm cotton tofu
- 2 garlic cloves, sliced
- 1 teaspoon salt
- 200g dried soba noodles
- 1 tablespoon olive oil
- 1 head of broccoli, weighing around 200g, roughly chopped
- salt and freshly ground black pepper
- 1 tablespoon toasted sesame seeds
- a big handful of shredded nori

A really simple lunch for when you haven't got much in the fridge — so much better than grabbing a sandwich from the local shop, with all those hidden fats and nasties!

Wrap the tofu in sheets of kitchen paper and leave it to drain on a slightly tilted chopping board for 20 minutes. Place a plate with a little weight on top of the tofu to speed up the draining. Or, if you are really pressed, microwave on medium for 1 minute. Then roughly chop the tofu.

Put the garlic and salt in a saucepan with plenty of water to bring to the boil over a medium heat. Cook the garlic for 2–3 minutes before adding the broccoli to cook for a further 3 minutes. Drain (but reserve a ladle of cooking water) and rinse under cold running water and drain well.

Meanwhile, bring another saucepan of water to the boil, add the noodles and stir to separate the strands. When the water comes back to the boil and begins to rise to the top, pour in a glass of cold water. Let the water return to the boil for a third time, drain, rinse under cold running water and drain again.

Put the olive oil in a frying pan to heat over a medium heat. Add the garlic, broccoli and tofu and, with a back of fork, squash the garlic and broccoli and add the reserved cooking water. When the broccoli mixture begins to bubble, add the soba noodles and stir to incorporate the noodles with the broccoli mixture. Season with the salt and pepper and divide between two serving plates. Garnish with the sesame seeds and shredded nori and serve immediately with chopsticks.

Salmon roe & grated daikon soba noodles

Serves 2

- 1 white or red onion, finely sliced
- 200g daikon, scrubbed clean
- 4 tablespoons salmon roe
- 1 tablespoon sake
- 200g dried soba noodles (preferably green tea-infused soba)
- 4 tablespoons Onion Soy-Dashi Sauce (page 40)
- 2 teaspoons wasabi powder, mixed with 4 teaspoons water

Daikon has become easier to find in supermarkets. It is a low-calorie vegetable rich in vitamins, particularly in A and C, and is known as a natural digestive. It also has a refreshing astringent taste. The easiest and the most effective way to get the full benefits is to eat it raw. Choose one that feels tight and solid, with no bruises.

Start by soaking the onion slices in a bowl of cold water to reduce their aroma and refresh. Grate the daikon, skin and all. Squeeze gently in your hand, fluff up the pulp and keep the juice to dilute the onion soy-dashi sauce. Mix the salmon roe with the sake.

Bring a saucepan of water to the boil, add the noodles and stir to separate the strands. When the water comes back to the boil and begins to rise to the top, pour in a glass of cold water. Let the water return to the boil for a third time, drain, rinse under cold running water and drain again.

Drain the onion slices. Divide the soba noodles between two serving plates and pour over the diluted onion soy-dashi sauce. Arrange the onion, grated daikon and salmon roe on top of each bowl. Serve with a small mound of wasabi paste in the middle and chopsticks.

Today life seems so hectic we barely have time to sit down for lunch. We are often forced into grabbing a pre-packed sandwich from the shop. While better than no lunch at all, a shop-bought lunch can be pretty doubtful — it's high in calories and fat, and above all, you have no control over the quality of the ingredients.

It takes only a little forward planning to make yourself a delicious and healthy packed lunch that will sustain you until the evening, as you'll discover with these recipes. Many recipes from the preceding chapter of One-bowl Lunch can also be used as moveable meals.

Lunch on-the-go

Rolled sushi

Serves 1

- a sheet of nori
- 80g prepared sushi rice (page 132)
- a small bowl of water
- wasabi paste

For the filling, choose from the following and cut into pencil-size strips
- fresh or cooked vegetables such as cucumber, carrot, asparagus or green beans
- sashimi-grade fresh fish such as tuna, salmon, sea bass or plaice
- smoked salmon

Equipment
- rolling mat

Rolled sushi is an ideal food-to-go. The rolling technique may seem a little tricky initially to those who are unaccustomed but with a little perseverance and practice, rolling sushi will soon become as easy as making sandwiches. The key to successful rolling sushi is to make sure you have all the ingredients and equipment at hand and are organised.

Halve a sheet of nori and place it on a rolling mat, smooth and shiny-side face down, in front of you. Wet your hands in the bowl of water, take the prepared sushi rice and form it into a sausage shape.

Place the rice on the nori and spread it evenly over the nori, leaving a 1cm margin along the top edge. The margin is for the overlap.

With your right index finger, smear a line of the wasabi paste across the centre of the rice and place a piece of filling (which you have cut into pencil-size strips) on top.

With both of your thumbs and index fingers, lift up the near side edge of the rolling mat while keeping the filling in place with your middle and third fingers. Bring the near side edge of the rice to meet the top edge of the rice and roll.

Open the rolling mat to reveal a roll, cover the roll with the mat again and gently run your hands along from the centre to the outer edges to shape the roll into a neat cylinder.

To cut a rolled sushi, place it on a chopping board, wet the blade of a sharp kitchen knife and cut it in half. Put the two halved rolls next to each other, in parallel, and cut them into three equal length pieces. You should now have six perfectly sized, rolled sushi pieces.

Stuffed sushi

Serves 1

For the seasoned, deep-fried tofu pouches
- 2 deep-fried tofu pouches
- 100ml water
- 1 tablespoon sugar
- 2 tablespoons soy sauce
- 1 tablespoon mirin

For the deep-fried, tofu-stuffed sushi
- 4 seasoned, deep-fried tofu pouches
- 1 tablespoon sushi pickled ginger, finely chopped
- 2 teaspoons toasted sesame seeds
- 160g prepared sushi rice (page 132)

Sweet, seasoned, deep-fried tofu is the classic choice for stuffed sushi. Although ready-made seasoned, deep-fried tofu pouches are available and they are a handy store cupboard standby, I always prefer the home-made ones. The seasoned tofu will keep for 4–5 days, if refrigerated, or for up to a month, if frozen.

Cut the deep-fried tofu pouches in half and pour boiling water over them to get rid of any excess oil. Carefully separate each half deep-fried tofu to make a pouch. Put all the tofu pouches in a saucepan with the water and sugar. Bring to the boil and cook for 3 minutes over a medium-high heat.

Add the soy sauce and mirin and reduce the heat to low to simmer until most of the liquid has evaporated.

To make the deep-fried, tofu-stuffed sushi, gently pat dry the tofu pouches to get rid of any excess liquid. Mix the sushi ginger and the sesame seeds with the sushi rice and divide into four equal portions. With a moist tablespoon, put the rice in each tofu pouch and fold over the top edge to enclose.

Salmon furikake (sprinkles)

Furikake (sprinkles) are very easy to prepare and make a healthy accompaniment to rice in a bento box (Japanese lunch box). Dry-frizzle the ingredients in a frying pan to remove any moisture.

Rub the salt over the salmon flesh, refrigerate for 30 minutes and then grill to cook to your liking. Remove and discard the skin and then break the flesh into fine flakes with your hands.

Serves 1

- ½ teaspoon salt
- 100g salmon fillet
- 1 teaspoon light soy sauce
- 2 tablespoons toasted sesame seeds
- ½ sheet of nori, finely shredded
- 100g cooled, cooked rice (page 31)

Put the salmon flakes in a non-stick frying pan with the soy sauce and dry-frizzle while stirring with two pairs of chopsticks over a low heat until all the moisture has evaporated. Add the sesame seeds and nori. Mix well to incorporate and then let the sprinkles cool down.

Put the cooled rice in a bento box and cover with the cooled sprinkles.

Wakame and green tea furikake (sprinkles)

To store the sprinkles, transfer to a container to refrigerate. The sprinkles will keep for 7 days in the fridge.

With a pestle and mortar, finely grind both the dried wakame and the tea together.

Heat a non-stick frying pan over a low heat and then dry-frizzle the wakame and tea until the mixture becomes crispy. Add the sesame seeds and let the sprinkles cool down.

Serves 1

- 15g dried wakame
- 1 tablespoon green tea leaves (preferably high-grade gyokuro variety)
- 1 tablespoon toasted sesame seeds
- 100g cooled, cooked rice (page 31)

Put the cooled rice in a bento box and cover with the sprinkles.

Omusubi (rice balls)

Makes 1

- 2 teaspoons salt
- 100ml cold water
- 80g warm, cooked rice (page 31)
- a sheet of nori

For the filling, choose one of the following:

- umeboshi (pickled plums), stones removed
- takuan (yellow pickled radish), chopped
- ready-made pickles of your choice, excess liquid removed
- small pieces of grilled fish
- chopped smoked salmon

Omusubi is a popular and classic 'takeaway' food in Japan. Warm rice is neatly shaped into various shapes with a small amount of filling in the centre, wrapped or covered with different dry ingredients. The choices of fillings and wrapping materials are almost endless. Once you have mastered the technique, I'm sure you will enjoy both making and eating omusubi. Here is how to make triangular omusubi, wrapped in nori. Usually the rice surrounds the filling, but as in the photograph you can make them so you can see the filling on one side.

In a bowl, dissolve the salt in the water. Moisten both hands with the salt water.

Rreserving a dessertspoonful of the warm, cooked rice, put the remaining rice on your left palm and gently squeeze. Make an indentation in the centre, put a filling of your choice (an umeboshi/pickled plum is the classic choice) and cover the filling with the reserved rice. With your right index and middle finger cupped over the rice in your left hand, shape into a neat triangle.

Cut a sheet of nori into two triangles. Place the omusubi on one of the triangle nori sheets. Bring up the bottom edge of the nori to cover the omusubi. Fold both left and right edges of the nori over the sides of the omusubi, leaving only the top tip of the omusubi uncovered.

Fresh spring rolls

Serves 2

- 4 sheets of rice paper, soaked in water to soften
- 1 baby cucumber
- 1 small carrot
- ½ avocado
- 2 tablespoons yofu (tofu yogurt)
- 1 teaspoon medium-colour miso paste
- ½ teaspoon wasabi paste
- 100g cooked prawns
- 4 lettuce leaves, trimmed

Rice paper is made from rice flour; it is low in calories and has no fat. It is also very quick and easy to use which makes rice paper ideal for making a quick lunch to go.

Pat the rice paper sheets dry and keep them separated in layers of moistened kitchen paper while you prepare the vegetables.

Cut the cucumber in half lengthways, cut them again lengthways and then discard the soft centre part. Peel the carrot and cut into four pencil thickness sticks. Cut the avocado into four strips. Mix the yofu with the miso and wasabi pastes.

Put the rice paper on a clean chopping board. Lay the lettuce, cucumber, carrot, avocado and prawns on top. Spoon the yofu mix over the vegetables and roll. Repeat the process to make four spring rolls. Cut each spring roll in half diagonally and pack in lunch boxes.

You may be surprised to know that salads are not part of the traditional Japanese cooking repertoire. Instead, Japanese cuisine has *sunomono* (literally 'vinegared things') and *aemono* ('combined' or 'harmonised' things). Small portions of *sunomono* and *aemono* are normally served as side dishes in elegant bowls. There is great scope for creativity in incorporating the traditional Japanese techniques of sunomono and aemono using ingredients such as rice vinegar, soy sauce and miso. All of the following recipes are designed as one-course meals either for lunch or supper. Some recipes are more filling than others and you need to adjust the balance between lunch and evening meals. Many recipes using daikon can easily be made more substantial by increasing the amount of daikon as it is 95 per cent water and has a very low-calorie count. And of course, if you do find yourself feeling peckish there is always the delicious guilt-free snacks to help you through in the Hunger Busters chapter.

Salads

Potato, green bean, tomato & spinach salad with minty soy dressing

This is the kind of salad lunch I enjoy eating on a warm day. It is beautiful to look at and full of summer garden tastes.

Cut the potatoes into thick slices and boil for 10 minutes. Blanch the beans for 2–3 minutes, refresh under cold running water and set aside to drain well. Soak the onion slices in a bowl of cold water for 10 minutes to rid it of its smell and drain.

Rub the garlic on the surface of a salad bowl or a serving plate. Mix all the ingredients for the dressing together.

Put all the vegetables in a salad bowl or on a serving plate, pour in the dressing, toss, sprinkle the sesame seeds and serve with chopsticks.

Serves 2

- 6 baby new potatoes, scrubbed clean
- 100g fine green beans, trimmed and halved
- $1/2$ red onion, thinly sliced
- 1 garlic clove, halved
- 10 baby vine tomatoes, halved
- 100g small spinach leaves, washed and drained
- 1 teaspoon toasted sesame seeds

For the minty soy dressing
- 4 tablespoons soy sauce
- 1 tablespoon runny honey
- 1 tablespoon rice vinegar
- 1 teaspoon sesame oil
- a handful of fresh mint leaves, finely shredded

Asparagus, green beans & hijiki soba noodle salad

This is one of my favourite combinations of tastes and textures. The sesame dressing brings all of the ingredients together, making it a satisfying one-course salad.

Bring a saucepan of water to the boil, add the noodles and stir to separate the noodles. When the water comes back to the boil and begins to rise to the top, pour in a glass of cold water and the hijiki. Let the water return to the boil, drain, rinse under cold running water and set aside to drain well.

Put the beans in another saucepan of water, bring it to the boil and cook for 2–3 minutes before adding the asparagus to cook for 1 minute. Drain and refresh with cold running water and drain well again.

To make the dressing, put the sesame seeds in a mortar, grind them to a rough texture, add the rest of the ingredients and grind to a smooth texture.

Put the noodles, vegetables and the dressing in a bowl and stir to mix. Divide into two equal portions, arrange on serving dishes, garnish with the sesame seeds and serve with chopsticks.

Serves 2

- 200g dried soba noodles
- 2 tablespoons dried hijiki
- 100g green beans, trimmed and halved lengthways
- 10 spears of asparagus, cut in the same length pieces as the beans
- 1 teaspoon toasted sesame seeds

For the sesame dressing
- 2 tablespoons toasted sesame seeds
- 1 tablespoon light brown sugar
- 2 tablespoons soy sauce
- 1 teaspoon miso paste

Mixed beans & bean sprouts with chilli sesame soy dressing

This is another easy and quick recipe using beans and bean sprouts. Serve warm in the cold season or chilled in the summer.

Cook the broad beans and carrot in a saucepan of boiling water for 2–3 minutes and drain.

In a separate saucepan of boiling water, blanch the bean sprouts and drain well. Drain the tinned beans and rinse under either cold or hot water, depending on how you are serving the dish.

Mix all the ingredients for the dressing together. Put the beans, sprouts, carrot and onion in a mixing bowl, pour in the dressing and mix well to dress. Divide the bean mixture between two serving dishes and serve either warm or chilled, with chopsticks.

Serves 2

- 75g broad beans, fresh or frozen
- 1 carrot, peeled and diced
- 100g bean sprouts, roots trimmed off
- 200g tinned mixed beans of your choice (drained weight)
- $1/2$ red onion, finely chopped

For the chilli sesame soy dressing
- 2 spring onions, finely minced
- 2 tablespoons soy sauce
- 1 teaspoon sesame oil
- 1 teaspoon runny honey
- 1 tablespoon toasted sesame seeds, ground
- $1/4$–$1/2$ teaspoon chilli pepper

Quick-pickled spring cabbage with sweet vinaigrette

Serves 2

- 4–6 large leaves of spring cabbage, roughly chopped into bite-size pieces
- 1 carrot, peeled and sliced
- ½ postcard-size piece of konbu, cut into thin and small strips
- ½ teaspoon salt
- 50g lotus root
- 10 mangetout, halved diagonally

For the sweet vinaigrette
- 2 tablespoons rice vinegar
- 1 tablespoon runny honey
- 1 teaspoon light soy sauce

Spring cabbages, especially pointed-head varieties, are tender and have mild sweet tastes that are best enjoyed fresh in salads.

Put the cabbage, carrot and konbu in a bowl, sprinkle the salt over, and squeeze and mix with your hands.

Fill another bowl – which fits inside the first bowl – with water, and sit it on top of the cabbage mixture for 30 minutes. Cut the lotus root chunk lengthways and slice thinly in half-moon shaped or quarter slices. Blanch the mangetout.

Mix all the ingredients for the sweet vinaigrette.

Squeeze the cabbage with your hands to rid it of excess water, add the mangetout and lotus root, pour in the vinaigrette and mix well. Set the mixture aside for 10 minutes or so to let the flavour develop before serving.

Tip
Outside of Japan, you are likely to come across lotus root already cooked in water and sold vacuum-packed – they have a relatively long shelf life and are easy to use. If you don't use it all up, keep refrigerated in a fresh bowl of water for up to a week.

Daikon, edamame & avocado salad with yuzu vinaigrette

This is one of my favourite salads because it is not only eye-catchingly beautiful but combines so many ingredients that are all good for your health and skin.

With a Japanese mandolin, shred the daikon and carrot into a big bowl of ice-cold water. Peel and halve the cucumber lengthways. Discard the seedy core and shred like the daikon and carrot.

Slice the red onion as thinly as possible into the bowl. With your hands, gently mix the daikon, carrot, cucumber and onion and refrigerate for at least 30 minutes while you prepare the other vegetables.

Cook the edamame in boiling water for 2 minutes, drain, cool under cold running water and leave aside to drain further. Cut the peppers into thin julienne and discard any white fibre or seeds. Drain the daikon mixture and divide between two serving plates and scatter the peppers on top of the daikon salad.

Halve, stone and peel the avocado, then cut into small cubes and arrange on top of the daikon salad. Sprinkle the edamame and pomegranate on top. Mix all the ingredients for the vinaigrette, drizzle it over the salad mixture and serve with chopsticks.

Serves 2

- 200g daikon, scrubbed clean
- 1 carrot, scrubbed clean
- 1 baby cucumber
- 1 small red onion, peeled
- 100g frozen edamame
- $1/2$ red pepper
- $1/2$ yellow pepper
- 1 avocado
- Seeds of 1 promegranate, plus any juice

For the yuzu vinaigrette
- 2 teaspoons yuzu juice
- 2 tablespoons rice vinegar
- 1 tablespoon light soy sauce
- 1 tablespoon runny honey

Tip
Yuzu is a yellow tangerine-like citrus fruit, of which the skin and juice are used to flavour food. Outside of Japan, the juice is sold in small bottles, which you should keep well-refrigerated, once opened. If you can't find it, use lime juice instead.

Tofu, crabmeat & avocado salad with wasabi dressing

Silky tofu and creamy avocado have a delicious affinity that is highlighted by the wasabi-based dressing. The recipe works equally well with tinned skipjack tuna or cooked prawns.

Wrap the tofu in sheets of kitchen paper and refrigerate for 30 minutes to drain naturally.

Soak the onion in a bowl of cold water to rid it of its smell. Cut the avocado into bite-size fan shaped slices and drizzle the lime juice to stop it from discolouring. Cut the tofu into bite-size slices of about 5mm thickness and arrange on a large serving platter.

Mix all the ingredients of the wasabi dressing. Drain the onion and put on top of the tofu, followed by the avocado and crabmeat. Drizzle the wasabi dressing, garnish with parsley leaves and serve with chopsticks.

Serves 2

- 200g soft silken tofu
- 1/2 white or red onion, thinly sliced
- 1 avocado
- juice from 1/2 lime
- 100g white crabmeat
- a few sprigs of flat leaf parsley

For the wasabi dressing
- 1 teaspoon wasabi paste
- 1 tablespoon light soy sauce
- 1 tablespoon rice vinegar
- 3 tablespoons extra-virgin olive oil

Tofu Caesar salad

We all know how good and healthy tofu is, although many people think it tastes bland. But it is exactly this blandness that makes tofu an ideal ingredient to cook with other foods. Think of tofu as a white canvas, ready for you to create a delicious culinary painting.

Wrap the tofu in sheets of kitchen paper and microwave on medium for 1 minute. Leave the tofu wrapped and let it cool down on more sheets of kitchen paper. Set aside to cool and further drain while you prepare the other ingredients.

Divide and arrange the salad leaves and watercress between two dishes. Mix all the ingredients for the salad dressing in a jar and shake it well to incorporate.

Cut the tofu into 2.5cm cubes. Heat the oil in a pan and fry the bacon and tofu until they become crispy. Remove the bacon and tofu with a slotted spoon on to kitchen paper first before arranging them on top of the salad leaves. Drizzle over the salad dressing, and serve with chopsticks.

Serves 2

- 200g firm cotton tofu
- 1 tablespoon vegetable oil
- 50g crunchy salad leaves like the Cos variety, roughly chopped
- 25g watercress, trimmed
- 2 rashers of streaky bacon, chopped

For the salad dressing
- 1/2 teaspoon grated garlic
- 1/2 tablespoon lemon juice
- 1/2 egg yolk
- 2 anchovy fillets, finely mashed
- 2–3 drops of Worcester sauce
- 2 tablespoons extra-virgin olive oil
- salt and freshly ground black pepper

Tofu salad

Serves 2

- 200g firm cotton tofu
- ½ white or red onion
- 1 baby cucumber
- 1 carrot, scrubbed clean
- 50g iceberg lettuce, finely shredded
- 6 radishes, thinly sliced
- 50g watercress, washed and trimmed
- 2 teaspoons toasted sesame seeds

For the salad dressing
- 2 tablespoons toasted sesame seeds
- 20g tofu (taken from the above)
- 2 tablespoons rice vinegar
- 1 tablespoon soy sauce (preferably light soy sauce)
- 1 teaspoon sugar
- ½ teaspoon sesame oil
- 2–3 tablespoons water

In this recipe, tofu is used twice – as a main salad ingredient and as a base for the dressing.

Wrap the tofu in sheets of kitchen paper and microwave on medium for 1 minute to rid it of the excess water (nearly 90% of tofu is water). Leave the tofu wrapped and let it cool down on more sheets of kitchen paper.

Meanwhile, slice the onion as thinly as possible and soak in cold water to rid it of its smell. Peel and halve the cucumber lengthways, discard the seedy core and julienne it, along with the carrot.

To make the dressing, put the sesame seeds in a mortar and grind them to a coarse texture. Add a 20g piece of tofu and continue to grind until the mixture becomes smooth. Add the rest of the dressing ingredients and adjust the consistency with the water.

Break the tofu into bite-size pieces with fingers and divide them into two equal portions. Drain the onion slices and divide all the vegetables into two equal amounts. Arrange half the tofu pieces on a serving plate and add (in this order) lettuce, carrot, cucumber, radishes, watercress and onion slices. Pour the dressing over the salad, garnish with the sesame seeds and serve with chopsticks.

Japanese ceviche of plaice with grapefruit & wild rocket

Ceviche is not Japanese. In fact, it is a speciality of the Central and South American Spanish-speaking countries. But there are similar ways of 'cooking' raw fish with citrus fruits and rice vinegar in Japan.

Run your fingers over the fillet to feel if there are any bones left and pluck them out with fish tweezers as necessary. Cut the fillet lengthways and slice diagonally across the grain of the flesh as thinly as possible.

Serves 2

- 200g plaice fillet, boned and skin removed
- 4 tablespoons frozen edamame
- 2 big handfuls of wild rocket leaves
- 1 grapefruit, peeled and segmented
- 1 tablespoon extra-virgin olive oil
- 1 tablespoon light soy sauce
- 1 teaspoon mixed black and white toasted sesame seeds
- 1/2 teaspoon chilli flakes

For the ceviche marinade
- 2 tablespoons rice vinegar
- 1 teaspoon yuzu juice
- 2 limes, finely grated zest and juice

To make the marinade, mix the rice vinegar, yuzu juice and lime juice and zest in a shallow dish. Add the fish slices. Cover with clingfilm and refrigerate to marinate for 1–1½ hours. The colour of the fish should turn from translucent to opaque white as it 'cooks' in the citrus marinade.

Meanwhile cook the frozen edamame in boiling water for 2 minutes, rinse under cold running water, drain and set aside to drain and cool further.

Divide the rocket leaves between two serving plates and arrange the grapefruit and edamame. Take the fish slices out of the marinade and pat dry with kitchen paper. Place and arrange them over the salad mixture. Drizzle the olive oil over the salad mound, followed by the soy sauce. Garnish with the sesame seeds and chilli flakes and serve with chopsticks.

Classic salmon sashimi with daikon salad

Serves 2

- 200g sashimi grade organic salmon fillet

For the daikon salad
- 200g daikon, scrubbed clean
- 1 baby cucumber
- 1 tablespoon black sesame seeds

For wasabi and sushi ginger dressing
- 1 tablespoon sushi pickled ginger
- 1/2 teaspoon wasabi powder
- 2 tablespoons soy sauce
- 2 teaspoons rice vinegar
- 2 tablespoons water

A cardinal principle of Japanese cuisine is that any seafood fresh enough to be eaten raw, should be served raw. Why cook when you don't need to? Preparing sashimi is a highly skilled job that is probably best left to professionals. In Japan, sashimi is sold already prepared, but I am pleased to see increasing numbers of fishmongers are selling fresh sashimi-grade seafood and are able to prepare at least a part of it. The freshness of the salmon is paramount.

You need a Japanese mandolin for this recipe, but it is an inexpensive kitchen implement that is sold in good kitchen shops or department stores.

Using the mandolin, shred the daikon into a large bowl of ice-cold water. Peel and halve the cucumber lengthways. Discard the seedy core and shred the cucumber into the bowl. Carefully mix the daikon and cucumber together and refrigerate for at least 30 minutes while you prepare the fish.

Ask your fishmonger to skin the salmon. Run your fingers over the fillet to feel if any bones remain, and pluck them out with fish tweezers as necessary. Trim off any brown meat as thinly as possible. Slice the fillet diagonally and across the white lines of the flesh into 1cm thick, double stamp-size rectangular pieces.

With a small blender, blend all the ingredients for the dressing until smooth. Drain the daikon and cucumber salad mixture and divide into two equal portions. Make a mound on a serving plate, garnish with black sesame seeds and arrange the salmon pieces beside it. Drizzle the dressing sauce (or use as a dipping sauce) and serve with chopsticks.

Salt salmon & noodle salad

In Japan, salmon is usually sold salt-cured. A little bit of salt on salmon really highlights the taste and texture of the fish. You have to think ahead to prepare the salt salmon I am afraid but I am most confident that you will enjoy the result.

Serves 2

- 1 teaspoon salt
- 200g salmon fillet, skin on
- 200g dry soba noodles
- 100g mixed salad leaves of your choice
- 2 spring onions, finely chopped diagonally
- 2 teaspoons toasted sesame seeds, roughly ground

For the dressing
- 2 tablespoons extra-virgin olive oil
- 2 tablespoons rice vinegar
- 1 tablespoon soy sauce
- 1 teaspoon sesame oil

On the night before you serve it, rub the salt all over the salmon, loosely wrap it in kitchen paper, place on a plate and refrigerate overnight. The fish should feel drier and stiffer to touch on the next day. Place the fish in a saucepan, add enough cold water to cover and slowly bring to the boil over a medium heat. Do not let it come to a rapid boil. Adjust the heat, simmer for 10 minutes and remove the fish from the water to cool down.

Meanwhile, bring a saucepan of water to the boil, add the soba noodles and stir to separate. Add a glass of cold water when the water returns to the boil and begins to rise to the top. Let the water come back to the boil for a third time, drain and rinse under cold running water. Leave aside to drain well and with a pair of kitchen scissors chop the noodles into manageable lengths. Put the salad leaves and soba in a salad bowl and gently toss to distribute evenly. Mix all the ingredients for the dressing. With your hands, remove and discard the salmon skin and break the salmon into bite-size pieces. Scatter the fish pieces and spring onions on the salad mixture, drizzle the dressing, sprinkle the sesame seeds and serve with chopsticks.

Smoked salmon, daikon & cucumber salad with watercress dressing

Smoked salmon is a wonderful ingredient; accessible and tasty, it can turn an ordinary bowl of salad into something quite special. Crisp daikon and a peppery watercress dressing beautifully counterbalance the rich oily taste and texture of the salmon.

Serves 2

- 500g daikon, peeled
- 1 carrot, peeled
- 1 baby cucumber

With a mandolin, shred the daikon into a large bowl of ice-cold water. Discard the top and the bottom of the carrot and shred as you did with the daikon. Peel and halve the cucumber lengthways, discard the seeds and shred. Mix the vegetables and place in the fridge for 30 minutes to crisp.

- a handful of rocket leaves
- 100g smoked salmon, torn into manageable length strips

For the watercress dressing
- 50g watercress, roughly chopped
- 2 tablespoons light soy sauce
- 2 tablespoons rice vinegar
- 1 teaspoon light brown sugar
- 1 teaspoon black sesame seeds
- 2 tablespoons sunflower oil

Meanwhile put all the ingredients for the dressing into a blender and mix until smooth.

Drain the daikon mixture well, divide into two equal portions and arrange on serving dishes. Put the rocket leaves on the daikon and arrange the salmon strips on top, drizzle the dressing over and serve with chopsticks.

Scallop sashimi with daikon salad

Scallops are high in protein, low in calories and rich in vitamin B2, which helps to metabolise sugar and fat — a great diet food. I love scallops, not only for their health benefits but also for their subtle sweet taste and plump succulent texture. They are particularly good in cold months. I urge you to try this recipe with the freshest 'hand-dived' varieties.

Serves 2

For the daikon salad
- 200g daikon, scrubbed clean
- 1 carrot, scrubbed clean
- 1 baby cucumber

- 4 scallops, shelled
- 1 spring onion, finely chopped
- a few sprigs of coriander leaves
- 1 teaspoon mixed black and white toasted sesame seeds
- 2 teaspoons wasabi powder, mixed with 1 tablespoon water
- 2 tablespoons tamari or soy sauce

With a mandolin, shred the daikon into a large bowl of ice-cold water. Discard the top and the bottom of the carrot and shred as you did with the daikon. Halve the cucumber lengthways, discard the seeds and shred. Mix the vegetables and place in the fridge for 30 minutes to crisp.

Clean the scallops as necessary, removing and discarding the orangey grey roe. Rinse under cold running water and pat dry with kitchen paper. Slice each scallop horizontally into three pieces.

Drain the daikon salad and divide between two serving plates. Arrange 6 pieces of scallop so that they overlap one another and place them on top of the daikon salad. Scatter the spring onion and coriander leaves and sprinkle the sesame seeds on top. To serve, make two small mounds of wasabi and place them on the side of each plate. Serve with small dipping dishes of soy sauce to the side, and chopsticks.

Squid salad with soy vinegar dressing

Serves 2

- 200g squid, skin and ink sac removed
- 2 tablespoons rice vinegar
- 100g red or speckled lettuce leaves
- 1 baby cucumber
- ½ red onion, thinly sliced

For the soy vinegar dressing

- 2 tablespoons soy sauce
- 2 tablespoons rice vinegar
- 1 garlic clove, grated
- 1 teaspoon grated fresh root ginger
- 1 tablespoon runny honey
- ½–1 teaspoon finely minced red chilli
- a few drops of sesame oil
- a small handful of torn fresh mint leaves

Squid is a popular choice of seafood in the Japanese diet. It is well-liked for its mild taste and unique texture. Nutritionally, squid contains less protein than the average fish, but it is easier to digest. It is also lower in fat and low-calorie; but its most notable feature is its rich taurine content (two to three times more than fish), which is an amino acid valued for lowering blood pressure and cholesterol as well as promoting a healthy liver.

Start by mixing all the ingredients for the dressing together to allow it to develop flavour.

Cut the squid body in half lengthways and clean, removing any quills. Score a shallow criss-cross pattern on the inside of the squid to prevent it from curling up, taking care not to cut all the way through the flesh. Cut it into 2.5cm square pieces. Cut the tentacles into bite-size pieces. Bring a saucepan of water to the boil over a moderate heat and add the rice vinegar. Poach the squid for 30 seconds, or until it turns opaque, and remove it with a slotted spoon.

Tear the lettuce leaves with your hands into 4–5cm pieces. Peel and halve the cucumber lengthways and discard the seeds. Slice thinly, diagonally. Put the squid, lettuce, onion and cucumber in a large bowl, add the dressing and toss to mix. Divide between two shallow dishes, garnish with the mint leaves and serve with chopsticks.

Smoked mackerel, broccoli, green bean salad with miso sesame dressing

This salad combines multiple layers of distinct tastes and flavours and is ideally served warm in cold months. Mackerel is often undeservedly under-rated. It is a very healthy food containing high levels of unsaturated fatty acids of both eicosapentaenoic acid (EPA) and docosa-hexaenoic acid (DHA). EPA cleanses the blood and helps to prevent arteriosclerosis as well as maintaining healthy eyesight, while DHA helps to maintain healthy brain cells and helps to lower cholesterol. Mackerel is plentiful and cheap and should be eaten more often!

Run your fingers over the fleshy side of the mackerel to feel any bones and remove them using fish tweezers as necessary. Peel the skin off and, with your hands, break up the flesh into small chunks and set aside.

Cut the broccoli and cauliflower into small, bite-size pieces. Cut the carrot into chunky slices. Bring a saucepan of water to the boil and cook all the vegetables, except the spinach, for 2 minutes. Drain, drizzle over the oils and keep warm.

With a pestle and mortar grind and mix together the ingredients for the dressing. Add the spinach leaves to the vegetables and gently mix to let the spinach wilt with the heat.

Divide the vegetable mixture between two serving plates. Arrange the mackerel on top, drizzle over the dressing and garnish with the spring onions and sesame seeds. Serve with chopsticks.

Serves 2

- 200g smoked mackerel fillet
- 100g broccoli
- 100g cauliflower
- 1 carrot, scrubbed clean
- 100g green beans, trimmed
- 2 big handfuls of salad spinach leaves
- 2 tablespoons sunflower oil
- a few drops of sesame oil
- 2 spring onions
- 1 teaspoon toasted sesame seeds

For miso sesame dressing
- 4 tablespoons toasted sesame seeds, ground
- 1 tablespoon soy sauce
- 1 teaspoon miso paste
- ½ teaspoon grated garlic
- 1 teaspoon runny honey
- 1 tablespoon rice vinegar

Prawn & sweet pepper salad with chilli soy dressing

This salad is not only beautiful on the table, it is packed with goodness to improve health and beauty. Prawns are low in calories and fat and have high taurine content, known to lower cholesterol and blood pressure. Sweet peppers have twice the vitamin C of lemon juice, which is great for beautiful skin. Peppers also have vitamin P, which helps to absorb vitamin C.

Serves 2

- 75g daikon, peeled
- 1 carrot, scrubbed clean
- 1 red or orange pepper
- 1 yellow pepper
- 200g ready-to-eat, cooked, medium-size prawns
- 100g baby spinach leaves
- 2 teaspoons toasted sesame seeds, roughly ground

For the chilli soy dressing
- 3 tablespoons rice vinegar
- 2 tablespoons soy sauce
- 1 tablespoon runny honey
- 2 teaspoons chilli sauce
- 1 teaspoon grated ginger juice
- 1 grated garlic clove
- a few drops of sesame oil

Put all the ingredients for the dressing in a small jar with a lid and shake well to mix. Set aside to marry the flavours.

Cut both daikon and carrot into thin 5cm long strips and soak in a bowl of cold water to refresh. Cut and deseed the peppers and thinly slice them. Drain the daikon and carrot.

Put the daikon, carrot, peppers and prawns in a bowl, pour on half the dressing and then toss thoroughly to evenly distribute, and dress.

To assemble the salad, make a bed of spinach on two plates and place the prawns and vegetable mix on top. Drizzle the remaining dressing over, sprinkle the sesame seeds, and serve with chopsticks.

Tuna, avocado & spinach salad with wasabi dressing

I was highly tempted to use seared tuna steaks for this recipe — but I decided to save them for later in this book. A lunch salad recipe should be simple, quick and easy to prepare with what you can find in your kitchen cupboard and fridge. But by no means should it be a mean affair.

Put the tuna, capers, onion, avocado and tomato in a big mixing bowl and gently mix together.

Mix all the ingredients for the wasabi dressing together and add to the tuna mixture. Put the spinach in a separate bowl and heat the olive oil in a stainless-steel spoon over a moderate heat, and pour over to wilt the spinach.

Divide and place the spinach between two plates. Spoon the tuna mixture on top of the spinach beds, garnish with the spring onions, top with the shredded nori and serve with chopsticks.

Serves 2

- 170g tinned skipjack tuna, drained
- 1 tablespoon capers, rinsed, drained and finely chopped
- $\frac{1}{4}$ white or red onion, finely minced
- 1 avocado, peeled, stone removed and diced
- 1 beef tomato, roughly chopped
- 100g baby spinach leaves
- 2 tablespoons olive oil
- 2 spring onions, finely chopped diagonally
1 sheet nori, finely shredded

For the wasabi dressing

- 2 teaspoons wasabi powder, mixed with 2 tablespoons water
- 1 tablespoon runny honey
- 1 tablespoon rice vinegar
- 2 tablespoons light soy sauce

Leftover chicken, cucumber & soba noodle salad with spicy miso & sesame dressing

Serves 2

- 200g dried soba noodles
- 50g fine green beans, trimmed
- 1 teaspoon sesame oil
- ½ white or red onion
- 1 baby cucumber, peeled
- up to 150g leftover roast chicken, shredded
- 2–3 tablespoons sushi ginger, finely shredded
- 50g mixed salad leaves
- 1 spring onion, finely chopped diagonally
- 1 teaspoon black sesame seeds

For the spicy miso and sesame dressing
- 4 tablespoons toasted white sesame seeds, finely ground
- 1 tablespoon sugar
- 1 tablespoon light-coloured miso paste
- 2 tablespoons soy sauce
- 1 tablespoon rice vinegar
- 1–2 teaspoons chilli sauce (depending on your taste)

This is what I call 'Let's see what's left in the fridge for lunch'. In my house, it happens quite regularly on Mondays after a family roast chicken on Sunday. The vegetables are only meant to be a guide. You can improvise with what you have in your own fridge.

Bring a saucepan of water to the boil, add the soba noodles and stir to separate the strands. When the water comes back to the boil again and begins to rise to the top add a glass of cold water. Add the fine green beans and let the water return to the boil. Drain and rinse under cold running water. Drain well again and drizzle with the sesame oil.

Slice the onion as thinly as possible and soak in cold water to refresh and rid it of the smell. Cut the cucumber into 5cm long chunks and chop into fine matchstick pieces, but discard the seedy core.

Mix all the ingredients for the spicy miso and sesame dressing.

Drain the onion slices. Put the noodles, beans, cucumber, onion, chicken and sushi ginger in a big mixing bowl. Pour over the dressing and toss gently to coat.

Divide the salad mixture into two equal portions, arrange on serving plates, top with the salad leaves, sprinkle the chopped spring onion and sesame seeds and serve with chopsticks.

Vegetable & chicken salad with sesame miso sauce

This is a big salad lunch I love to eat on an early spring day, when the weather is not quite warm enough. As I'm sure you know, steaming the chicken and vegetables is a really healthy cooking method.

Cut the cabbage, broccoli and chicken into bite-size pieces. Arrange the carrot, leek and the chicken in a steaming basket. Drizzle over 2 tablespoons of sake and steam over a high heat for 8 minutes.

Arrange the cabbage, broccoli and mangetout in a separate steaming basket. Drizzle over the rest of the sake, place the basket underneath the first basket and steam for 2–3 minutes.

Mix together all the ingredients for the sesame miso sauce and adjust the thickness with 1–2 tablespoons water.

Arrange the vegetables and chicken on a warm serving platter, drizzle over the sauce and serve warm with chopsticks.

Serves 2

- 200g pointed-head spring cabbage
- 100g sprouting broccoli
- 2 chicken mini fillets
- 1 carrot, peeled and sliced diagonally
- 1 leek, trimmed and sliced diagonally
- 4 tablespoons sake
- 100g mangetout

For the sesame miso sauce

- 3 tablespoons toasted white sesame seeds, finely ground
- 2 tablespoons light-coloured miso paste
- 1 tablespoon sugar
- 3 tablespoons rice vinegar
- 1 teaspoon grated ginger juice

Shredded chicken salad with creamy tofu dressing

Tofu is a food that never seems to stop dividing opinions. But whatever your view of tofu, this is a tasty way of using it.

Place the chicken fillets in a saucepan and cover them with plenty of water. Bring to the boil and cook them for 5 minutes. Take the chicken out and let it cool down before shredding it with a fork.

Bring a separate saucepan of water to the boil. Put the tofu in a sieve and submerge in the water for 2–3 minutes. Take it out and drain. Using the same boiling water, cook the spinach for 1 minute, refresh in a bowl of cold water and drain well.

Put the tofu in a mixing bowl and squash it to a smooth paste with the back of a spoon. Add the ground sesame and sesame oil, mix well to combine, and season with salt and pepper. Mix in the chicken and spinach. Divide the salad mixture into two portions, transfer to two dishes and serve with chopsticks.

Serves 2

- 2 chicken mini fillets
- 100g soft silken tofu, broken into large pieces
- 100g spinach, roughly chopped
- 1 tablespoon toasted sesame seeds, finely ground
- 2 teaspoons sesame oil
- salt and white pepper

Beef carpaccio & aubergine with ginger dressing

This is an adaptation of a classic Italian carpaccio of beef with a Japanese twist, both in taste and the method used. I also like to try this recipe when I get hold of fresh spring lamb loin fillet.

Preheat the grill to the highest setting. Prick the aubergine all over and place under the grill for about 20 minutes to brown the skin and cook the aubergine flesh. Slice the beef fillet into strips, as thinly as possible. Take a length of clingfilm, about 60cm long, and fold it over. Place a slice of the beef about one-third of the way from the left-hand side of the clingfilm, fold it over the beef to cover, and with a rolling pin start to gently smash the meat out, working from the centre to outwards, until wafer thin.

Mix all the ingredients for the ginger soy dressing together. Peel off the aubergine skin, roughly chop and divide the flesh into two equal portions. Make mounds of aubergine in the centre of two plates. Arrange the beef slices around the mounds, put the rocket leaves on top, drizzle the dressing, garnish with the spring onion and sesame seeds, and serve with chopsticks.

Serves 2

- 1 aubergine
- 100g beef fillet
- 50g wild rocket leaves
- 1 spring onion, finely chopped
- ½ teaspoon toasted sesame seeds

For the ginger soy dressing
- 2 teaspoons grated ginger juice
- ½ small garlic clove, grated
- 2 tablespoons soy sauce
- 1 tablespoon extra-virgin olive oil

Seared beef, rocket & grapefruit with wasabi dressing

This classical way of cooking meat or fish is called 'tataki', which means to beat or hit – you slap the meat with the palm of your hand to flatten and tenderise it. Choose as good quality beef as you can get for the best result.

Take the beef out of the fridge and let it come to room temperature, because cold meat is tough and takes longer to cook. Put a heavy-based frying pan over a high heat. Pat the beef dry with kitchen paper, brush with the sesame oil and brown for 1–2 minutes on each side, depending on the thickness of the meat and your preference. Transfer the meat onto a chopping board, sprinkle the rice vinegar over it, and let it rest.

Meanwhile, peel off the membrane from the grapefruit segments, divide the rocket leaves between two serving plates and arrange the grapefruit around them. Mix all the ingredients for the dressing together. With a sharp knife, cut the meat into thin slices. Separate the slices and give each a light but firm slap with the palm of your hand. Arrange the beef slices on top of the salad, drizzle the dressing, sprinkle the sesame seeds and serve with chopsticks.

Serves 2

- 125g sirloin/fillet beef, fat trimmed
- ½ teaspoon sesame oil
- 2 tablespoons rice vinegar
- 1 grapefruit, peeled and segmented
- 100g wild rocket leaves
- 1 tablespoon toasted sesame seeds

For the wasabi dressing
- 1 teaspoon wasabi powder, mixed with 1 teaspoon water
- 1 tablespoon runny honey
- 2 tablespoons rice vinegar
- 2 tablespoons light soy sauce

Crispy duck with orange & watercress salad

Serves 2

- 1 duck breast
- $1/2$ teaspoon salt
- 1 orange or blood orange
- 100g watercress

For the dressing
- 2 tablespoons orange juice
- 1 tablespoon soy sauce
- 2 teaspoons rice vinegar
- 2 teaspoons wasabi powder

The key to achieving a really crispy duck skin is to ensure the skin is dry before cooking, so take the breast out of its wrapping in advance. Duck is often seen as fatty but in this recipe most of the fat is drained off to make the crispy skin and we use only one breast to make two servings. So don't be put off and enjoy this delicious salad with a clear conscience!

With a fork, prick the duck breast, rub the salt on to the skin and set aside to draw out the moisture. Grate the orange for its zest, separate the segments and carefully remove all the membrane.

Heat a heavy-based frying pan over a medium heat, place the duck skin-side down and cook for 5 minutes to render the fat. Remove the duck and discard any fat, return the pan to the heat and turn up the temperature to high. Put the duck back in the pan skin-side up for 2 minutes to seal and turn it over on the skin side for 3–5 minutes, or until the skin is crisp and golden. Remove the duck on to a plate lined with kitchen paper, skin-side up, to rest.

Mix all the ingredients for the dressing with the orange zest. Divide and arrange the watercress and orange segments on two serving plates. Cut the duck into thin slices and arrange them over the salad mixture, drizzle over the dressing, and serve with chopsticks.

The simplest and most quintessential Japanese meal is rice with a bowl of soup and a few slices of pickled vegetables. In Japanese cuisine, soups are the most important side dish to accompany rice; in fact, in a formal meal with several courses, both clear broth-based and miso-flavoured soups are served at both ends of the meal. Miso-based soups with a variety of seasonal ingredients make a quick and easy, healthy one-bowl meal. Despite the growing westernisation of eating habits, millions of Japanese still begin their day with a bowl of miso soup for breakfast and finish it with another bowl at the end of the day.

Miso is made of fermented soy beans and other grains such as rice, wheat and barley. The colour of miso ranges from pale cream to steely, dark brown and the colour is a rough indication of taste — the lighter the colour, the less salty the taste. But this is a rather simplistic generalisation and doesn't begin to describe the rich and complex tastes, flavours and aromas of miso. Miso is a very healthy food — the soy bean's high-quality protein is converted into easily digestible amino acid. Miso helps to lower cholesterol and blood pressure, it is also anti-cancerous, anti-oxidant and anti-ageing. Although by no means conclusive, much research shows that Japanese women suffer no or fewer menopausal symptoms, linked, it is believed, to their higher intake of soy protein such as tofu and miso. Recent research has revealed that soy beans contain several phenolic compounds called isoflavones that resemble the human oestrogen hormone and provide similar health benefits.

Remember, soups are also eaten with chopsticks in Japan. Eat the meat and vegetables with chopsticks and then pick up the bowl with both hands to drink the soup.

Soups

Dashi

A good bowl of soup starts with delicious dashi — Japanese stock. Compared to its western counterpart, dashi is a quick and easy-to-prepare stock. The quality of dashi is particularly important for miso soups in which miso is almost the sole seasoning ingredient. I have listed four methods of making dashi at the beginning of this section.

Primary dashi

- 2 postcard-size pieces of konbu, wiped clean, with incisions made into them
- 600ml water
- 25g dried bonito fish flakes

This is a finely balanced dashi that is most suitable for clear soups and miso soups with vegetables with delicate aromas.

Place the konbu in a saucepan with the water and leave for 20 minutes to infuse. Heat the saucepan over a medium heat, taking care not to let it reach the boil and remove the konbu pieces when they begin to float to the top and bring to a full boil. Add the bonito fish flakes. There is no need to stir. Immediately turn off the heat and let the fish flakes settle at the bottom. Filter through a cheesecloth-lined sieve. Reserve the bonito flakes and konbu for making Secondary Dashi (see below).

Secondary dashi

- reserved konbu and bonito fish flakes from the Primary Dashi (see above)
- 5g bonito fish flakes
- 600ml water

While Primary Dashi is best suited to clear soups by virtue of its aroma, delicate flavour and clarity, Secondary Dashi, with its more robust taste, makes a good base for miso soups with seafood or root vegetables.

Put the reserved konbu and fish flakes, along with the fresh fish flakes in a saucepan with the water and heat over a medium heat. Remove the konbu when the water begins to boil and continue to cook until the water is reduced by 10 per cent. Like Primary Dashi (see above), filter through a cheesecloth-lined sieve.

Vegetarian dashi

- 2 postcard-size pieces of konbu, wiped clean, with incisions made into them
- 3 dried shiitake mushrooms
- 1 litre water, boiled and cooled

Here is a vegetarian version of dashi that is very subtle and suitable for gentle vegetable soups.

Put all the ingredients together in a bowl with the water and leave to infuse at a room temperature for 3–4 hours in cooler months, or 2–3 hours in the summer. The dashi will keep up to a week, refrigerated.

Anchovy dashi

- 30g dried anchovies, heads and entrails removed, halved lengthways
- 2 postcard-size pieces of konbu, wiped clean, with incisions made into them
- 600ml water

Water dashi

- 2 postcard-size pieces of konbu, with incisions made into them
- 30g dried anchovies, heads and entrails removed
- 2 dried shiitake mushrooms
- 1 litre water, boiled and cooled

Dashi no moto (instant granular dashi)

Miso

Tips for making a good miso soup

This is a type of fish stock made with very small, silvery, sun-dried anchovies. Savoury anchovy dashi is much stronger than primary or secondary dashi, made with bonito fish flakes, and it makes a very tasty base for thick and rich miso soups.

Put the prepared anchovies and the konbu in a saucepan with the water and leave it to infuse for 20 minutes. Put the saucepan over a medium heat and slowly bring to just under the boil while removing any foam from the surface and cook for 5–6 minutes. Turn off the heat and filter through a cheesecloth-lined sieve.

With no cooking involved, this is by far the easiest method for making a reliable, basic dashi.

Put all the ingredients together in a lidded jar and refrigerate overnight. The dashi will keep for up to a week, refrigerated.

This is a dry granular form of dashi made by manufactures that is widely used in Japanese kitchens. Think of it as a Japanese equivalent of a stock cube, in other words, a convenient storecupboard standby to be used sparingly.

To enjoy miso's rich and complex tastes and unique flavour, never boil it for a long time. Add it only when all the other ingredients in the soup are cooked through and let the soup return to the boil only for 1 second before turning off the heat. A rough guide to the amount of miso paste per person is between a tablespoon and a heaped tablespoon.

You can enrich and deepen the flavours of miso soup by blending two or three different varieties of miso paste. Use paler and less salty ones to create comforting blends in colder months and use darker varieties to make a refreshing flavour in the summer. You can create your own favourite blends by experimenting and combining different varieties of miso pastes. Do not put a wad of miso paste directly into the soup and expect it to dissolve on its own. Always use a ladleful of the soup liquid to soften the paste in a small bowl first or use a small, fine-mesh sieve and the back of a wooden spoon to push it through into the soup.

Chilled miso soup of aubergine, tomato, edamame & cucumber

For those who think that miso soup is always served hot, here is a refreshing, chilled miso soup to enjoy during the summer. I suggest serving it in a chilled glass bowl. Aubergines are low in calories and help to reduce cholesterol. They also contain polyphenol, found in red wine too, which helps to lower blood pressure, and is anti-ageing and anti-cancerous. Although aubergines are available throughout the year, they are at their best in the summer and early autumn.

Serves 2

- 1 medium aubergine
- 6 baby vine tomatoes
- 1 tablespoon vegetable oil, for brushing
- 2 tablespoons frozen edamame
- 300ml Dashi (page 106) – primary, water or vegetarian
- 1 baby cucumber, thinly sliced
- 2 tablespoons light-coloured miso paste
- 1 shallot, peeled and thinly sliced
- a small handful of flat-leaf parsley

Preheat a heavy, cast-iron griddle to high. Cut off and discard the stem of the aubergine, halve lengthways and slice diagonally into thick chunks. Brush the aubergine and tomatoes with the oil and place on the hot griddle to brown the surfaces. At the same time, cook the edamame in a small saucepan of boiling water for 2 minutes, drain and set aside.

Put the aubergine in a saucepan with the dashi. Place over a medium heat to cook for 5 minutes, taking care not to let it come to the boil. Add the tomatoes, edamame and cucumber. Cook for a further 2 minutes.

Put the miso paste in a small bowl and add a ladleful of the soup liquid to soften and dissolve the paste. Pour it into the saucepan. Turn up the heat and let the soup come to the boil for 1 second and then quickly turn off the heat. Let the soup cool to room temperature, before refrigerating it for 1 hour.

Meanwhile, soak the shallot slices in a bowl of cold water to rid them of their smell. Drain. Stir the soup and ladle it into two chilled bowls. Arrange the shallot on top, garnish with the parsley and serve with chopsticks.

Chilled misopacho

Serves 2

- 1 baby cucumber, peeled, seeded and roughly chopped
- 2 large, very ripe tomatoes, roughly chopped
- 1/2 small red onion, roughly chopped
- 1/4–1/2 large red chilli, de-stemmed and seeded
- 2 teaspoons fresh root ginger
- 1 garlic clove
- 100ml tomato juice
- juice of 1 lime
- 2 tablespoons rice vinegar
- 2 tablespoons soy sauce
- 1 tablespoon extra-virgin olive oil
- 1 tablespoon red miso paste
- salt and freshly ground pepper
- 6 baby vine tomatoes, halved
- 1 celery stick, strings removed and diced
- 2 teaspoons extra-virgin olive oil
- a few sprigs of coriander

I first came across gazpacho over three decades ago now. I instantly fell in love with it and have been making it ever since. This is my latest version, with a few Japanese twists. Miso paste brings an extra depth of flavour to the soup, without overpowering it.

Put the cucumber, tomatoes, onion, chilli, ginger and garlic in a food processor or a blender to purée. Add the tomato juice, lime juice, rice vinegar, soy sauce, oil and miso paste. Purée until smooth and well blended. Adjust the seasoning.

Transfer to a large bowl, cover with clingfilm and refrigerate for at least 4 hours, but preferably overnight, to allow the flavours to fully develop.

Divide the soup between two chilled bowls, top with baby tomatoes and diced celery. Drizzle the olive oil and garnish with coriander.

Grilled aubergine & sweet pepper miso soup with ginger mustard

Serves 2

- 1 medium aubergine
- ¹/₂ red pepper
- ¹/₂ yellow pepper
- ¹/₂ green pepper
- ¹/₂ tablespoon vegetable oil
- 15g fresh root ginger, peeled and grated
- ¹/₂ tablespoon English mustard
- 300ml Dashi (page 106) – primary, water or vegetarian
- 1 tablespoon medium-coloured miso paste
- 1 tablespoon red- or dark-coloured miso paste

Ginger has long been used in traditional Chinese medicine as well as a popular ingredient in all Asian cooking. It is a natural steriliser, increases the body's metabolism, aids digestion and encourages perspiration. And further more, recent findings show that ginger also helps to reduce cholesterol and lowers blood pressure.

Preheat the grill. Prick the aubergine all over. Line a baking tray with tinfoil and place the aubergine on it to grill for 20 minutes. Turn it over halfway through to brown the other side.

Chop the peppers into bite-size pieces and brush with the oil. Add the peppers to the aubergines and grill for a further 10–15 minutes or until the aubergine is browned all over and the peppers are cooked.

Meanwhile, mix the grated ginger with the mustard and set aside to develop flavour. Transfer the aubergine on to a plate and with a bamboo skewer, peel off the skin and cut into bite-size pieces. Divide the vegetables between two bowls.

Put the dashi in a saucepan and bring to the boil over a medium heat. Put both of the miso pastes in a small bowl and ladle in the dashi to soften and dissolve the pastes. Pour it back into the saucepan. Turn up the heat to let the soup come to the boil for 1 second. Ladle into the two bowls, topped with a dab of ginger mustard. Serve with chopsticks.

Japanese mushroom miso soup

The mild, warm and moist climate of the Japanese archipelago makes it a treasure house for mushrooms of all varieties and Japanese people love mushrooms. Mushrooms have vitamin D, which helps the body to absorb calcium, and vitamin B2, otherwise called the beauty vitamin because it metabolises fat and sugar as well as lowering cholesterol levels in the blood. Mushrooms are also rich in edible fibres and above all, they are low calorie food so try and get into a habit of using them.

Put the mushrooms in a saucepan with the dashi and bring them to the boil over a medium heat.

Put the miso pastes in a small bowl, ladle in the dashi to soften and dissolve the pastes. Then pour back into the saucepan. Add the wakame, turn up the heat and let it come to the boil for just 1 second. Ladle between two bowls, garnish with the spring onions and serve immediately with chopsticks.

Serves 2

- 200g Japanese mushrooms such as shiitake, shimeji, enoki and maitake, choosing at least two different varieties (see Tip)
- 300ml Dashi (page 106) – primary, water or vegetarian
- 1 tablespoon light-coloured miso paste
- 1 tablespoon medium-coloured miso paste
- 2 tablespoons dried wakame, softened in water and drained
- 2 spring onions, finely chopped diagonally

Tips

Depending on which mushrooms you choose, here are some tips for preparing them to make bite-size pieces. For shiitake, discard the stalks and slice the caps. When preparing shimeji and enoki mushrooms, discard the bases of both and then separate the mushrooms with your hands. For maitake mushrooms, discard the bases and tear the delicate lacework-like mushrooms into manageable pieces with your hands.

Creamy roast pumpkin miso soup

Pumpkin is a very healthy vegetable. It is rich in beta-carotene, which becomes Vitamin A, once digested. It strengthens the skin's mucous membrane to protect the body from infectious diseases. Pumpkin also contains twice as much vitamin C as tomatoes and has one of the highest vitamin E contents. Vitamin E is an effective anti-oxidant and helps to slow down the ageing process. Roasting draws out the delicious, natural sweetness of pumpkins. I'm going to allow you to eat this one with a spoon! But remember to take your time to eat and appreciate this health-giving soup.

Serves 2

- 400g kabocha or buttercup (green skin) pumpkin
- 1 tablespoon vegetable oil, for brushing
- ½ teaspoon salt
- 1 teaspoon grated fresh root ginger
- 300ml Dashi (page 106) – primary, water or vegetarian
- 2 tablespoons white- or light-coloured miso paste
- 1 teaspoon toasted sesame seeds

Preheat the oven to 200°C/400°F/Gas Mark 6. Cut the pumpkin into four wedges. Discard the seeds, brush with the oil, sprinkle with the salt and place on a roasting tray, skin-side down, to roast for 45 minutes or until very tender.

Scoop the flesh from the skin and put it in a saucepan. Mash until very smooth. Add the ginger and the dashi and stir until even. Place the saucepan over a high heat to cook until it boils.

Put the miso paste in a small bowl, ladle in a small amount of the soup liquid to soften and dissolve the paste. Pour it back into the saucepan and turn up the heat to let it come to the boil for 1 second. Ladle into two bowls, sprinkle over the sesame seeds and serve immediately.

Spinach & burdock miso soup with maitake mushrooms

Serves 2

- 100g burdock, scrubbed clean
- 50g maitake mushrooms
- 100g spinach, washed and drained
- 300ml Dashi (page 106) – primary, secondary, water or vegetarian
- 1 tablespoon light-coloured miso paste
- 1 tablespoon medium red-coloured miso paste
- 1 teaspoon toasted sesame seeds

The Japanese are the only nation to eat burdock, a long and slim root vegetable. The burdock's main component is a non-digestible carbohydrate, which creates the feeling of being satisfied, and also provides a unique, crisp texture and flavour. Recent research shows that the lignin that is found just under the surface is anti-cancerous, discharges cholesterols, and prevents arteriosclerosis and diabetes. Therefore, clean them by scraping off the outer layer of skin rather than peeling off the entire skin. Burdock is a healthy ally for slimmers. Frozen bags of sliced burdocks are available from Japanese stores.

Soak the burdock in water for 10–15 minutes and drain well. Cut and discard the base of the maitake mushrooms and tear into bite-size pieces with your hands. Chop the spinach into 5cm lengths. Put the burdock in a saucepan with the dashi and bring to the boil over a medium heat. Adjust the heat to simmer for 5 minutes. Add the maitake and spinach and cook for 3 minutes.

Put the miso pastes in a small bowl, ladle in a small amount of the soup liquid to soften and dissolve the pastes. Pour it back into the saucepan and turn up the heat to let it come to the boil for 1 second. Ladle the soup into two warm bowls, sprinkle with the sesame seeds and serve immediately with chopsticks.

Japanese corn chowder

Sweet white miso lends an exotic flavour to freshly crushed corn – a tasty marriage of East and West. I suggest serving chilled on warm Indian-summer days, or piping hot on dull and grey autumn days to provide comfort for both the body and soul.

Serves 2

- 200g soft silken tofu
- 1 fresh corn on the cob
- 1 teaspoon grated fresh root ginger
- 300ml Dashi (page 106) – primary, secondary, water or vegetarian
- 2 tablespoons mirin
- 2 tablespoons white miso paste
- pinch of salt
- ½ tablespoon sesame oil
- a few sprigs of fresh coriander, roughly chopped

Wrap the tofu in sheets of kitchen paper and leave it to drain on a slightly tilted chopping board for 20–30 minutes. If you are short of time, place a plate with a little weight on top of the tofu to speed up the draining. Or, if you are really pressed, microwave on a medium heat for 1–2 minutes.

Cook the corn, covered, in lightly salted boiling water for 10–12 minutes and strip the kernels from the cob. Put the corn in a food processor or blender and blend until coarsely smooth. Add the tofu and the ginger to blend until the mixture is uniformly smooth.

Put the corn mixture in a saucepan together with the dashi and mirin, over a high heat and bring to the boil. Reduce the heat to simmer for 5 minutes.

Put the miso paste in a small bowl, ladle in a small amount of the soup liquid to soften and dissolve the paste. Pour it back into the saucepan and turn up the heat to let it come to the boil for 1 second. Adjust the seasoning with the salt, if necessary. Ladle the soup into two bowls and drizzle over the sesame oil. Garnish with the coriander and serve with chopsticks.

Tofu, seaweed, carrot, leek & sprouting broccoli miso soup

Serves 2

- 100g firm cotton tofu
- 2 tablespoons dried wakame
- 300ml Dashi (page 106) – secondary, water or vegetarian
- 1 small carrot, peeled and sliced diagonally
- 1 leek, trimmed and sliced diagonally
- 100g sprouting broccoli, cut diagonally
- 1 heaped tablespoon light-coloured miso paste
- 1 heaped tablespoon medium-coloured miso paste
- 1 teaspoon toasted sesame seeds, ground roughly

This is a variation on a classic miso soup with tofu and wakame seaweed. A miso soup is generally made with two or three ingredients but I have added a few more late winter/early spring vegetables to create a nourishing one-course soup.

Wrap the tofu in sheets of kitchen paper and leave it to drain on a slightly tilted chopping board for 20–30 minutes. If you are short of time, place a plate with a little weight on top of the tofu to speed up the draining. Or, if you are really pressed, microwave on medium for 1 minute.

Meanwhile, to soften the wakame, soak it in a bowl of cold water for 10 minutes and drain. With the dashi, put the carrot and leek in a saucepan and heat it over a medium heat but make sure it does not reach a full boil. Simmer to cook for 5 minutes.

Cut the tofu into dice-size pieces; add the tofu, wakame and broccoli to the saucepan. Cook for 3 minutes. Put the miso pastes in a small bowl, ladle in a small amount of the soup liquid to soften and dissolve the pastes. Pour it back into the saucepan and turn up the heat to let it come to the boil for 1 second. Ladle the soup into two bowls, garnish with the sesame seeds and serve with chopsticks.

Caramelised onion miso soup with burnt tofu

This is the Japanese answer to the famous French onion soup. The secret to creating a deep-flavoured sweetness is to sauté the onion with lots of patience thrown in.

Whether you have burnt or normal, firm tofu, it needs to be well-drained. Wrap the tofu in sheets of kitchen paper and leave it to drain on a slightly angled chopping board for 20 minutes. Dice the tofu and set aside.

Serves 2

- 100g burnt tofu or firm cotton tofu
- 1 tablespoon vegetable oil
- 4 red onions, thinly sliced
- 4 tablespoons black rice vinegar or red wine vinegar
- 1 teaspoon sugar
- 1 tablespoon soy sauce
- 300ml Dashi (page 106) – secondary, water or vegetarian
- 1 tablespoon light-coloured miso paste
- 1 tablespoon red- or medium-coloured miso paste

Put the oil in a saucepan and sauté the onions for 15 minutes over a low heat, stirring constantly to prevent them browning. Add the vinegar, sugar and soy sauce and continue to cook until the liquid is reduced to almost nothing. Pour in the dashi and increase the heat to high to bring to the boil.

Put the miso pastes in a small bowl, ladle in a small amount of the soup liquid to soften and dissolve the pastes. Pour it back into the saucepan and turn up the heat to let it come to the boil for 1 second. Ladle into two bowls, top with the tofu and serve immediately with chopsticks.

Tip
Burnt tofu is firm cotton tofu that is scorched on the surface. If you are unable to find it, use a well-drained, firm tofu and grill or burn it with a food torch.

Leek and turnip miso soup with chicken

Serves 2

- 2 chicken thigh fillets, skin on
- 300ml Dashi (page 106) – secondary or water
- 1 medium leek, trimmed and sliced
- 1 turnip, peeled and cut into bite-size wedges
- 1 medium carrot, peeled and cut into thick slices
- 2 tablespoons white- or light-coloured miso paste

You will love this delicious combination of leek and turnip, two lovely winter vegetables that are sure to keep the cold at bay in the winter. Crispy chicken skin creates a tasty, contrasting texture, without adding too many calories to the bowl.

Peel the skin off the fillets, reserve and cut the flesh into bite-size pieces. Blanch the skin in boiling water, pat it dry and slice into thin strips. Put the chicken with the dashi in a saucepan and bring to the boil over a medium heat. Reduce the heat to simmer for 5 minutes.

Meanwhile, sauté the chicken skin in a small frying pan without any oil until it becomes crisp and set aside on kitchen paper to soak up any oil. Add the vegetables to the chicken dashi broth and simmer for another 5 minutes or until the vegetables are cooked through.

Put the miso paste in a small bowl, ladle in a small amount of the soup liquid to soften and dissolve the paste. Pour it back into the saucepan and turn up the heat to let it come to the boil for 1 second. Ladle the soup into two warm bowls, top with the crispy skin and serve immediately with chopsticks.

Pork miso soup with konnyaku

Serves 2

- 1 block of konnyaku
- 1 tablespoon sesame oil
- 50g belly of pork, thinly sliced
- 15g fresh root ginger, peeled and roughly chopped
- 1 carrot, peeled and roughly chopped
- 1 medium parsnip, peeled and roughly chopped
- 300ml Dashi (page 106) – secondary, water or vegetarian
- 6 mangetout, cut in half diagonally
- 1 tablespoon light soy sauce
- 1 tablespoon red- or medium-coloured miso paste
- 1 tablespoon light-coloured miso paste
- 1 tablespoon sushi ginger, roughly chopped
- 1 teaspoon toasted sesame seeds

Konnyaku means 'the devil's tongue' or 'elephant foot' in Japanese. Despite its unappealing name, it is a slimmer's dream food. This speckled, grey, gelatinous and elastic block is made from the root of the konnyaku plant. It has no fat, no calories and little taste. It works like a cleansing agent to rid the digestive system of cholesterols, impurities and waste matter. It is sold vacuum-packed with a little limewater. Combining konnyaku with meat is an effective way to reduce cholesterol.

With your hands, break the konnyaku into small bite-size pieces. Put the sesame oil in a saucepan, place it over a medium heat and sauté the pork for 3 minutes. Add the ginger, carrot, parsnip and konnyaku. Cook for a further 3 minutes.

Add the dashi and mangetout and let it come to the boil, scooping up any foam which floats to the surface. Reduce the heat to maintain a simmering temperature. Season with the soy sauce. Put the miso pastes in a small bowl, ladle in a small amount of the soup liquid to soften and dissolve the paste. Pour it back into the saucepan and turn up the heat to let it come to the boil for 1 second. Ladle the soup into two bowls and top with the sushi ginger. Sprinkle over the sesame seeds and serve immediately with chopsticks.

Asparagus, pea & new potato miso soup with salmon

Asparagus, new potatoes and peas all signal the beginning of summer. I like to eat them as much as possible during their all-too-short season. This recipe gives an unusual but delicious way of enjoying all those wonderful seasonal offerings.

Preheat the grill to high. Brush the salmon with the oil, season with salt and pepper. Place the salmon on a grilling rack skin-side down and grill for 5 minutes or until the flesh of the fish is browned. Take the fish out of the grill, and leave until it is cool enough to handle. Remove the skin and break into bite-size chunks with your hands.

Put the potatoes in a saucepan with the dashi to cook over a medium heat for 10 minutes, adjusting the heat, if necessary, so that the dashi does not reach boiling point. Add the peas, asparagus and salmon and continue to cook for a further 3 minutes.

Put the miso pastes in a small bowl, ladle in a small amount of the soup liquid to soften and dissolve the pastes. Pour it back into the saucepan and turn up the heat to let it come to the boil for 1 second. Ladle the soup into two bowls, garnish with pea shoots, if using, and serve immediately with chopsticks.

Serves 2

- 100g salmon fillet
- a few drops of vegetable oil, for brushing
- pinch of salt and freshly ground black pepper
- 100g new potatoes, scrubbed clean and thickly sliced
- 300ml Dashi (page 106) – secondary or water
- 60g fresh peas
- 6 asparagus spears, chopped diagonally
- 1 tablespoon light-coloured miso paste
- 1 tablespoon medium-coloured miso paste
- a small handful of pea shoots (optional)

Clam chowder miso soup with crispy deep-fried tofu

Serves 2

- 1 sheet of deep-fried tofu, defrosted if frozen
- 1 tablespoon vegetable oil
- 1 small red onion, finely minced
- 1 celery stick, finely chopped
- 100g new potatoes, scrubbed clean and roughly diced
- 200g bottled or tinned clams, drained
- 300ml Dashi (page 106) – secondary, water or anchovy
- 100ml soy milk
- ½ teaspoon agar agar, diluted in 2 teaspoons water
- 2 tablespoons light-coloured miso paste
- 1 spring onion, finely chopped diagonally
- 1 teaspoon toasted sesame seeds

This is a classic, creamy clam chowder with a Japanese twist.

Microwave the deep-fried tofu for 30 seconds on a medium heat to rid it of any excess oil. Cut it into stamp-size pieces. Dry-toast the deep-fried tofu in a small non-stick frying pan over a medium heat, shaking the pan regularly for 3–5 minutes or until the tofu becomes crisp. Transfer to kitchen paper and set aside until needed.

Put the oil in a large sauté pan, place on medium and sweat the onion for 3 minutes. Add the celery and potatoes and sauté for a further 3 minutes. Add the clams and continue to sauté for 2–3 minutes before adding half of the dashi.

Transfer the soup mix to a food processor or blender to blend – working in small batches, if necessary. Return the soup to the saucepan and add the remainder of the dashi and soy milk. Place the saucepan over a medium heat to bring it to just beneath the boil. Adjust the heat so that the soup does not reach the boil but remains just below. Simmer for 5 minutes.

Add the agar agar to thicken the soup. Put the miso paste in a small bowl, ladle in a small amount of the soup liquid to soften and dissolve the paste. Pour it back into the saucepan and turn up the heat to let it come to the boil for 1 second. Ladle the soup into two bowls, garnish with the crispy deep-fried tofu, spring onion and sesame seeds and serve with chopsticks.

Prawn & tomato miso soup with okra

Serves 2

- 6 medium fresh prawns with shells
- 300ml Dashi (page 106) – secondary or water
- 2 large, ripe vine tomatoes
- 6 okra, blanched, stems discarded and chopped into 5mm thick slices
- 1 tablespoon dark-coloured miso paste
- 1 tablespoon red-coloured miso paste

This is a visually stunning soup, which has added benefits for your skin because prawns contain an amino acid called taurine, so you will be visually stunning too!

Remove the heads from the prawns and shell them. Make a shallow slit along the back of the prawns to remove the veins. Put the heads and shells of the prawns in a saucepan with the dashi over a medium heat. Adjust the heat, if necessary, to ensure that the dashi continues to simmer just below the boiling point.

Meanwhile, cut a slit around the middle of each tomato. To remove the tomato skins, put them in boiling water for a few minutes and then peel off the skins. Cut in half horizontally to remove the seeds and chop into bite-size pieces.

With a slotted spoon, remove and discard the prawn heads and shells from the dashi. Add the prawns to cook for 3 minutes or until they turn pink and are cooked. Add the okra.

Put the miso pastes in a small bowl, add a ladleful of the dashi to soften and dissolve the pastes. Pour the miso back into the saucepan. Turn up the heat to let the soup boil for a second and then add the tomatoes. Ladle into two bowls and serve with chopsticks.

Let's be totally honest... how many times have you regretted eating a heavy dinner late in the evening, knowing that what you have just eaten will be an unspent energy source and may well cause you a disturbed night of sleep? A large evening meal is a particularly bad idea if you are trying to lose weight. But I have done this countless times because, apart from holidays and weekends, evenings are often the only time of day when I can really take time to enjoy cooking and relax together with my family and friends.

In this section, I have come up with delicious, low calorie and low fat, easy to digest, yet satisfying and comforting recipes to wind down the day, guaranteed to give you a good night's beauty sleep.

Light suppers

How to prepare sushi rice

Serves 2

- 200g Japanese-style short grain rice
- 220ml water
- 1 postcard-size piece of konbu

For the sushi vinegar mix

- 2 tablespoons rice vinegar
- 1 tablespoon sugar
- 1 teaspoon salt

Put the rice in a bowl, cover with cold water and stir quickly with your hands until the water becomes milky-white and then pour the water away. Repeat the process until the water runs clear.

Transfer the rice to a sieve and set it aside for at least 30 minutes or, ideally, for 1 hour. The resting is particularly important when preparing sushi rice because it allows the rice to absorb the moisture and plump up.

Put the rice in a tight-lidded, heavy-based saucepan – a small Le Creuset one is ideal. Add the water and the konbu, cover with the lid and bring to the boil over a medium-low heat.

Do not lift the lid but look out for thin steam escaping and listen for the bubbling sound. Increase the heat to high and cook for 3 minutes. Turn off the heat. Again, do not lift the lid but let it stand to steam for further 10–15 minutes.

For the sushi vinegar, mix all the ingredients in a non-metallic bowl and stir until all the sugar and salt are dissolved. Discard the konbu and transfer the cooked rice to a moistened, shallow, flat-based basin.

Sprinkle the sushi vinegar over the rice, and with a wooden spatula in a sideways cutting motion, toss the rice to coat with the vinegar until all the vinegar has been absorbed and the rice becomes glossy.

Fan the rice to cool while tossing – this is easier if you have someone else to stand by. The job is traditionally given to a young apprentice in a sushi restaurant in Japan. If you are not using the rice immediately, cover with a clean, damp cloth and eat on the same day. Sushi rice can be prepared up to 3 hours in advance but do not refrigerate.

Aubergine & broccoli sushi

Aubergines are almost calorie-free and the sponge-like flesh absorbs any taste or flavour you may wish to create — another great diet food. Although there are no particularly noteworthy nutrients, polyphenol that gives the aubergine its vibrant colour, is known to be anti-oxidant which helps to slow down the ageing process.

Serves 2

- 1 medium aubergine
- 6 sprouting broccoli, trimmed
- 200g prepared sushi rice (see opposite)
- 2 tablespoons sushi ginger, finely chopped
- 1 tablespoon toasted sesame seeds
- salt

Cut the aubergine into quarters lengthways and then cut them diagonally into bite-size, diamond-shaped pieces. Bring a saucepan of salted water to the boil and blanch the aubergine for 2 minutes. Drain into a sieve and sprinkle over a pinch of salt to revive the colour. At the same time, bring another saucepan of salted water to the boil, blanch the broccoli and drain. Put the sushi rice and the ginger in a bowl and mix to incorporate.

Divide the sushi rice mixture between two serving dishes and arrange the aubergine and broccoli on top, garnish with the sesame seeds and serve with chopsticks.

Bamboo shoot sushi

Bamboo shoots have few nutrients to speak of but they are high in edible fibre which makes them great for slimmers. Outside Japan, bamboo shoots are sold ready-prepared in water-filled vacuum packs.

Serves 2

- 100g bamboo shoots
- 1/2 deep-fried tofu pouch
- 1 chicken thigh fillet
- 200ml Dashi (page 106)
- 2 tablespoons soy sauce
- 2 tablespoons mirin
- 200g prepared sushi rice (see opposite)
- a small handful of shredded nori
- 1 tablespoon pickled sushi ginger, finely shredded

Take the bamboo shoots out of the pack, rinse briefly with water, pat dry and cut into bite-size pieces. Put the tofu pouch in a sieve and pour over boiling water to remove any excess oil. Pat dry and slice into small strips.

Remove and discard the chicken skin. Chop the chicken into small, bite-size pieces. Put the bamboo shoot, tofu and chicken in a shallow saucepan with the dashi, soy sauce and mirin. Bring to the boil over a high heat. Reduce the heat to simmer for 15–20 minutes until all the cooking juice has evaporated.

Put the prepared sushi rice in a bowl, add the bamboo mixture and stir to incorporate. Divide and transfer the sushi mixture to two serving dishes. Sprinkle over the nori, top with the sushi ginger and serve with chopsticks.

Smoked salmon sushi

Serves 2

- ½ white or red onion, finely sliced
- 200g prepared sushi rice (page 132)
- juice of 1 lime
- 2 tablespoons capers, finely chopped
- 50g smoked salmon, roughly chopped
- 2 big handfuls of wild rocket leaves
- 2 tablespoons salmon roe, mixed with 1 tablespoon sake
- 1 sheet of nori, torn into small pieces, to garnish

Sushi is such a delicious, light food – perfect for supper – and this colourful dish will make you forget you're on a diet. Use wild rocket if you can for the outstanding flavour, but obviously use normal rocket if you can't find it.

Start by soaking the onion slices in a bowl of cold water for 10 minutes (soaking rids the onion of the anti-social smell but retains the taste and crunchy texture) and drain.

Put the sushi rice in a bowl, sprinkle over the lime juice and mix with the capers.

Divide and transfer the rice to two serving plates and arrange the smoked salmon pieces and top with the rocket leaves. Scatter over the onion and spoon the salmon roe on top. Garnish with the nori pieces and serve with chopsticks.

Marinated tuna sushi

Serves 2

- 100g tuna steak, diced
- 200g prepared sushi rice (page 132)
- a handful of wild rocket leaves, roughly chopped
- 1 spring onion, finely chopped
- 1 punnet of cress
- 2 tablespoons toasted sesame seeds
- a handful of shredded nori

For the soy marinade
- 1 tablespoon toasted sesame seeds
- 1 spring onion, finely chopped
- 2 tablespoons soy sauce
- 1 tablespoon sake
- 2 teaspoons wasabi paste

This regional cuisine from Mie Prefecture (south-east of Nagoya) derives its Japanese name, tekone zushi, from the fact that the soy-marinated tuna is mixed with the sushi rice by hand. It is a very satisfying and tactile way to prepare a sushi. However, you can leave the tuna and rice separate if you wish.

Put the tuna in a non-metallic bowl with all the ingredients for the marinade and leave for 30 minutes. Remove the tuna from the marinade and pat it dry.

Put the prepared sushi rice in a flat-based basin and add the marinated tuna, rocket leaves, spring onion and cress. With your hands, mix the rice with the tuna and saladings to incorporate evenly. Divide and transfer the sushi mixture to two serving dishes. Sprinkle with the sesame seeds, garnish with the shredded nori and serve with chopsticks.

White crabmeat & pomegranate sushi

The pomegranate is called the 'fruity panacea' because of its anti-oxidant properties. It may help to protect the body from heart disease, premature ageing, Alzheimer's disease and cancer. The fruit originates in Persia and has been the subject of myths and works of art. In this stunningly beautiful and refreshing recipe, both the ruby-like fruit and the juice are used.

Serves 2

- 100g frozen broad beans (or fresh if in season)
- 200g prepared sushi rice (page 132)
- seeds from 1 pomegranate, plus any juice
- 100g ready-to-eat cooked white crabmeat
- 2 tablespoons fresh coriander, finely chopped
- 1 tablespoon fresh mint, finely chopped
- 1 tablespoon toasted sesame seeds

For the vinegar mix
- 2 tablespoons red wine vinegar
- 2 tablespoons pomegranate juice

Cook the broad beans for 3 minutes, drain, and peel the outer skin (it is fiddly, but the result is well worth the extra effort). Mix together the red wine vinegar and pomegranate juice for the vinegar mix.

Put the sushi rice in a mixing bowl, add the pomegranate, broad beans and crabmeat. Pour the vinegar mix over the rice mixture, and with a sideways cutting motion, toss the rice to incorporate.

Divide the sushi mixture on to two serving dishes, garnish with the coriander and mint leaves, and sprinkle over the sesame seeds. Serve with chopsticks.

Country-style kayu with chicken & miso

Serves 2

- 80g Japanese-style short grain or brown rice
- 100g chicken thigh fillet, fat removed and chopped into bite-size pieces
- 1 tablespoon sake
- 1 carrot, scrubbed clean
- 1 leek, trimmed
- ½ tablespoon sesame oil
- 50g frozen burdock (available from Japanese stores)
- 600ml Dashi (page 106) – secondary or water
- 2 shiitake mushrooms, stems discarded and caps sliced
- 4 mangetout, halved diagonally
- 4 tablespoon medium-coloured miso paste
- 2 spring onions, finely chopped diagonally
- 1 teaspoon toasted sesame seeds

Kayu is the Japanese word for 'rice porridge'. Its origin is believed to go back to the confines of a solemn Zen Buddhist temple where monks started their long, Spartan training days with a bowl of plain rice porridge and a few slices of pickles. The monks' breakfast, however, makes a perfect light supper. There are a few types of kayu, all defined by the ratio of liquid to rice. For a dieter's evening meal, I recommend the 'seven-portion kayu' which uses a ratio of seven portions of liquid to one portion of rice. This is a robust kayu, full of tastes and flavours that are guaranteed to leave you feeling satisfied and uplifted.

Wash and rinse the rice under cold, running water until the water runs clear and then set aside in a sieve to drain for at least 30 minutes. Put the chicken in a bowl and sprinkle over the sake.

Halve both the carrot and the leek lengthways and then slice them diagonally. Place a wok over a medium heat and add the sesame oil. When the wok is almost smoking hot, add the chicken and stir-fry for 3 minutes. Add the rice, burdock, carrot and leek and stir-fry for 2–3 minutes before pouring in the dashi. Let the dashi come to the boil, reduce the heat to medium-low, cover the wok with a lid and cook for 20 minutes.

Add the mushrooms and mangetout to the wok. Stir and cook for another 5 minutes. Put the miso paste in a big cooking ladle and submerge it in the rice to soften and dissolve, then add.

Add the spring onions and gently stir to incorporate all the ingredients into the wok before turning off the heat. Divide and spoon into two bowls, sprinkle the sesame seeds on top and serve immediately with chopsticks.

Dried shiitake mushroom kayu with spinach

This is an adaptation of a recipe originating in traditional Chinese medicine where a wide variety of dried mushrooms are used to boost the immune system. But you certainly don't have to be ill to enjoy this soothing yet satisfying kayu.

Wash and rinse the rice under cold, running water and set aside to drain in a sieve for at least 30 minutes. At the same time, put the shiitake mushrooms in a bowl and cover with enough boiling water to soften – reserve both the juice and the mushrooms.

Sprinkle the sesame oil over the rice and toss to coat before placing it in a heavy-based saucepan with the dashi. Drain and slice the shiitake mushrooms and add to the rice with the juice. Place the saucepan over a high heat to bring to the boil, reduce the heat to medium-low and continue to simmer for 25–30 minutes.

Season with the soy sauce and mirin. Add the spinach and stir to soften before turning off the heat. Divide and ladle into two warm bowls, garnish with the spring onion, sprinkle over the sesame seeds and serve with the chopsticks.

Serves 2

- 80g Japanese-style or brown rice
- 4 dried shiitake mushrooms caps
- ½ tablespoon sesame oil
- 560ml Dashi (page 106) – secondary, water or vegetarian
- 2 tablespoons soy sauce
- 1 tablespoon mirin
- 100g spinach, cleaned and roughly chopped
- 1 spring onion, finely chopped diagonally
- 1 teaspoon toasted sesame seeds

Wakame kayu with miso & shimeji mushrooms

I am sure that you won't be surprised to hear that there are literally countless ways of cooking and seasoning rice in Japanese cuisine. This is a healthy and tasty combination of seaweeds, mushrooms and miso paste that is sure to give you a comforting evening meal.

Wash and rinse the rice under cold, running water until the water runs clear and set aside in a sieve to drain for at least 30 minutes. Put the rice in a heavy-based saucepan with the dashi and bring to the boil, covered, over a high heat. When the rice reaches the boil and begins to boil over, lower the heat to simmer for 20 minutes.

Discard the base of the shimeji mushrooms and separate. Drain the wakame and add to the rice with the carrot and shimeji. Continue to simmer for a further 10 minutes. Add the spring onion.

Put the miso paste in a ladle and submerge into the rice to soften and dissolve, and stir to incorporate. Turn off the heat, ladle into two warm bowls and serve immediately with chopsticks.

Serves 2

- 80g Japanese-style or brown rice
- 560ml Dashi (page 106)
- 1 pack of shimeji mushrooms
- 1 tablespoon dried wakame, soaked in water
- ½ carrot, scrubbed clean and sliced diagonally
- 1 spring onion, finely chopped
- 2 tablespoons medium-coloured miso paste

White crabmeat kayu

When you manage to find crabmeat that is still in the shell, try this delicate but tasty kayu.

Wash and rinse the rice under cold, running water until the water runs clear and set aside in a sieve to drain for at least 30 minutes.

Serves 2

- 80g Japanese-style or brown rice
- 200g crabmeat in shell
- 100g Chinese cabbage, chopped
- 600ml Dashi (page 106) – secondary or water
- 2 tablespoons sake
- 1/2 teaspoon salt
- 2 tablespoons light soy sauce
- 1 egg, lightly beaten
- 2 spring onions, finely chopped diagonally

Meanwhile, shell the crab and pick out the crabmeat. Put the rice, crab shells and Chinese cabbage, along with the dashi, in a heavy-based saucepan and bring to the boil over a high heat.

When it is boiling and begins to boil over, reduce the heat to medium-low and cook for 25–30 minutes. Discard the crab shells and add the crabmeat. Season with the sake, salt and soy sauce and let it return to the boil.

Pour in the egg and stir to swirl. Turn off the heat when the egg begins to set. Ladle into two warm bowls, garnish with the spring onions and serve immediately with chopsticks.

Prawn & egg kayu

I believe everyone should have a few tasty recipes that can quickly be rustled up with what's in the fridge – and this is one of them.

Serves 2

- 80g Japanese-style or brown rice
- 100g frozen prawns
- 560ml Dashi (page 106) – secondary or water
- 1 1/2 tablespoons light soy sauce
- 1 1/2 tablespoons sake
- 2 eggs, lightly beaten
- a few sprigs of coriander leaves, roughly torn

Wash and rinse the rice under cold, running water until the water runs clear and set aside in a sieve to drain for at least 30 minutes.

Put the rice in a heavy-based saucepan with the prawns, dashi, soy sauce and sake. Place the saucepan over a high heat to bring to the boil. Reduce the heat to low to simmer for 20 minutes.

Pour in the eggs and stir to swirl. Cook for 3 more minutes before turning off the heat. Divide and spoon into two warm bowls. Garnish with the coriander and serve with chopsticks.

Oyster kayu

Serves 2

- 80g Japanese-style short grain or brown rice
- 10 fresh oysters, shelled
- 560ml Dashi (page 106) – secondary, anchovy or water
- ½ teaspoon salt
- 1 tablespoon light soy sauce
- 1 teaspoon grated fresh root ginger
- ½ lemon peel, thinly sliced
- a few sprigs of fresh coriander, roughly torn
- 1 sheet of nori, crushed into small pieces
- 1 spring onion, finely sliced

Kayu is very easy to digest and the ultimate comfort food and with the addition of some fresh oysters you can make your supper a little bit more glamorous! I have two different garnish options for this recipe: either with lemon peel, coriander and nori, or simply with some spring onion. It's up to you!

Wash and rinse the rice under cold, running water until the water runs clear and set aside in a sieve to drain for at least 30 minutes. Put the oysters in a sieve and briefly rinse under cold, running water. Set aside to drain.

Put the rice, dashi, salt and soy sauce in a heavy-based, cast-iron saucepan with a tight-fitting lid. Bring to the boil over a high heat and cook for 5 minutes. When it begins to boil over, adjust the lid and reduce the heat to medium-low to cook for 25–30 minutes.

Add the oysters, stir and let the rice return to the boil. Stir in the grated ginger before turning off the heat. Divide and ladle into two warm bowls. Garnish with the slices of lemon peel, the coriander and crushed nori or, for a simpler approach, some spring onion. Serve immediately with chopsticks.

Sea bream on rice

Serves 2

- 100g Japanese-style short grain rice
- 100g sea bream fillet
- ½ teaspoon salt
- 175ml Dashi (page 106) – primary or water
- 2 tablespoons light soy sauce
- 2 tablespoons sake
- ½ punnet of cress, to garnish

With its delicious taste, texture and appearance, sea bream is regarded as the king of fish in Japan. No auspicious feast is complete without this handsome fish. It has well-balanced, high-quality protein and is easy to digest.

Wash and rinse the rice under cold, running water until the water runs clear and set aside in a sieve to drain for at least 30 minutes.

Meanwhile, preheat the grill and cut the fish diagonally into bite-size slices 1.5cm thick. Sprinkle over the salt and set aside for 10 minutes. Grill the fish for 2 minutes on each side.

Put the rice in a heavy-based, shallow sauté pan with a solid lid. Add the dashi, soy sauce and sake. Cover with the lid and bring to the boil over a medium heat. Cook for 10 minutes or until the surface is free of the cooking liquid.

Spread the fish on top and cook for a further 5 minutes. Turn off the heat and let it steam for a further 10 minutes, before garnishing with the cress. Serve with chopsticks.

Three bean rice soup

Serves 2

- 150g Japanese-style short grain rice
- 50g pudding rice
- 300ml water
- ½ postcard-size piece of konbu
- 25g edamame
- 25g broad beans
- 25g green peas
- 2 tablespoons sake
- ½ teaspoon salt
- 1 teaspoon black, toasted sesame seeds

You may choose any combination of beans but this recipe is delicious with edamame, green peas and broad beans, which, usefully, are all now available frozen.

Start by rinsing both types of rice until the water runs clear. Put them in a heavy-based saucepan with a tight-fitting lid. Add the measured amount of water along with the konbu and cook over a gentle heat for 30 minutes.

Add the beans and peas, sake and salt. Replace the lid and bring to the boil over a gentle heat. Look out for signs that it has started to boil, such as bubbling sounds or thin ribbons of steam escaping from the pan, but do not lift up the lid to have a look.

Turn the heat up to high to cook for 3 minutes and then turn off the heat. Let it steam for a further 10 minutes before giving it a few stirs to fluff up the rice.

Divide into two bowls, sprinkle the black sesame seeds on top and serve with chopsticks.

Okonomiyaki (Japanese savoury pancake)

Serves 2

- 200g spring, pointed-head or Savoy cabbage, finely shredded
- 100g bean sprouts, trimmed
- 2 spring onions, finely chopped
- 25g grated fresh root ginger
- 4 tablespoons plain flour
- 1/2 teaspoon salt
- 2 eggs
- 1 tablespoon vegetable oil
- 4 rashers streaky bacon, roughly chopped in bite-size pieces
- 2 handfuls of bonito fish flakes
- 2 tablespoons Japanese okonomiyaki sauce (or brown sauce)
- 2 tablespoons shredded nori

Okonomiyaki is a popular snack that dates back 300 years to the streets of Tokyo. The main ingredients are shredded cabbage, eggs and seasoned flour, which acts as a binding agent. Cook it like a pancake on a hot plate.

Put the cabbage, bean sprouts, spring onions, grated ginger, flour, salt and eggs in a big bowl. Use a tablespoon to mix lightly, in cut-and-turn motions. Do not over-mix, as it will make the mixture sticky and heavy.

Place an omelette pan over a medium heat and add half the amount of oil. Pour half the mixture into the pan. Sprinkle over half the amount of bacon and put a handful of bonito fish flakes on top – the fish flakes will sway because of the heat, but do not press them down.

Cook for 5–6 minutes and turn it over to cook the other side for a further 6–7 minutes and then turn it over again to cook for 3 minutes. Remove from the heat and keep warm while cooking the second half of the cabbage mixture in the same way.

Transfer the cooked okonomiyaki onto two plates and spread over the Japanese okonomiyaki sauce using the back of a spoon. Sprinkle with the shredded nori and serve with chopsticks.

Courgette okonomiyaki with tuna

I created this version of the classic okonomiyaki one summer when there seemed no end of courgettes growing in my vegetable garden.

With a Japanese mandolin or grater, shred the courgettes, squeeze out the excess liquid and fluff up. In a big bowl, add all the ingredients except the oil. Mix and incorporate in a cut-and-turn motion but do not over-mix to avoid the mixture becoming too sticky and heavy.

Heat half the amount of oil in a frying pan over a medium heat. Divide the courgette mixture into two portions. Put one portion on the pan and gently spread the mixture to a dessert plate size but do not press down.

Cook one side for 6–7 minutes, then turn over to cook the other side for 5–6 minutes. Repeat the process to cook the other half of the courgette mixture. Transfer the okonomiyaki on to a serving plate, garnish with bonito fish flakes and serve with chopsticks.

Serves 2

- 4 courgettes, washed and trimmed
- 1 red pepper, seeded and finely sliced
- 1 red onion, finely sliced
- a big handful of flat leaf parsley, finely chopped
- 2 garlic cloves, grated
- 170g tinned tuna, drained and flaked
- 4 tablespoons plain flour
- 1 teaspoon chilli flakes
- 1/2 teaspoon salt
- 2 eggs
- 1 tablespoon vegetable oil
- a handful of bonito fish flakes

Salmon hotpot

Serves 2

- 4 tablespoons dried seaweed mix
- 200g daikon, scrubbed clean
- 1 carrot, scrubbed clean
- 450ml Dashi (page 106)
- 1 leek, trimmed and thinly sliced diagonally
- 100g Chinese cabbage, thinly sliced
- 1 garlic clove, grated
- 100g salmon fillet, sliced diagonally into bite-size pieces
- 4 tablespoons medium-coloured or red miso paste
- 1 tablespoon lemon juice

Hotpot is a great Japanese classic – family and friends sit around a big pot on the table, cooking seasonal or regional favourites. I have adapted it to make a healthy and tasty light supper that is easy to prepare by even the most reluctant cook.

Start by putting the seaweed mix in a bowl, cover with water and leave aside to soften. Cut the daikon into 1cm thick slices and quarter each slice. Chop the carrot into 1cm thick slices diagonally. Put the daikon and carrot in a saucepan with the dashi to bring to the boil over a medium heat.

Drain the seaweed mix, and when the dashi begins to boil, reduce the heat and add the seaweeds, leek, cabbage, garlic and salmon. Cook for 10 minutes. Put the miso paste in a small bowl, ladle in a small amount of the dashi to soften and dissolve the paste. Add to the saucepan. Increase the heat to let the dashi return to the boil for 1 second. Ladle into two warm bowls, drizzle over the lemon juice and serve with chopsticks.

Tofu hotpot

Serves 2

- 1 postcard-size piece of konbu
- 400ml water
- 200g soft silken tofu
- soy sauce
- a handful of bonito fish flakes
- a handful of spring onions, finely chopped

Tofu should not be cooked for a long time – it will develop small holes and become spongy. Think of warming the tofu rather than cooking it.

Place the konbu at the base of a saucepan, cover with the water and leave for 30 minutes to infuse.

Cut the tofu into 2.5cm cubes. Place the saucepan over a low heat to bring to the boil slowly. When small bubbles begin to appear, add the tofu to heat gently until the tofu cubes start to shake in the water. Turn off the heat and divide the tofu between two warm dishes. Serve with soy sauce, fish flakes and spring onions.

Warm salad of steamed plaice with creamy yofu dressing

Plaice is another slimmers' dream fish – it is rich in high-quality protein, low in fat and calories. It is also high in vitamin B1 and B2 that help to calm stresses and its rich vitamin D helps the absorption of calcium and prevents osteoporosis. Its delicately flavoured white flesh contains collagen that helps to maintain youthful skin. The best season for plaice is during the cold months and early spring – so having it in a warm salad is a perfect way to enjoy this wonderful fish.

Serves 2

- 200g plaice
- 4 tablespoons sake
- salt and freshly ground black pepper
- 200g purple-sprouting broccoli
- 6 spears asparagus
- 4 heaped tablespoons broad beans
- 10 fine beans, trimmed

For the creamy yofu dressing
- 4 tablespoons toasted sesame seeds, grounded
- 6 tablespoons yofu (tofu yogurt)
- 1 tablespoon runny honey
- 2 tablespoons soy sauce
- 1/2 teaspoon sesame oil

You need 2 bamboo steaming baskets for this recipe. Cut the fish into manageable bite-size pieces. Put it in a shallow dish that fits into the bamboo steaming basket, pour in the sake and season with salt and pepper.

Cut the broccoli into bite-size pieces. Discard the lower parts of the asparagus and cut them into half lengths.

Put the fish dish in a bamboo basket with the lid on and place it over a saucepan with enough water to steam over a moderate heat for 10–12 minutes.

Mix all the ingredients for the creamy yofu dressing while the fish is steaming.

Put the fine beans in another basket, leaving enough room for the other vegetables and put the basket underneath the fish basket. Continue to steam for 2 minutes before adding all the other vegetables to steam for another 2 minutes.

Divide all the ingredients into two equal portions and arrange them on two serving dishes. Pour the dressing over each dish and serve with chopsticks.

Japanese rolled cabbage

Serves 2

- ½ head Chinese cabbage
- 200g lean pork mince
- ½ onion, finely minced
- ½ carrot, finely minced
- 1 teaspoon grated fresh root ginger
- 1 egg yolk
- ½ teaspoon salt and pepper
- 3 teaspoons cornflour
- 200ml Dashi (see page 106)
- 2 tablespoons soy sauce
- 4 teaspoons water
- a few fresh mint leaves, very finely shredded

I used to be and am still somewhat averse to using the microwave oven, so it stood as one of the most under-used items in my kitchen. But I am beginning to think again. The microwave is quick, clean and simple, especially when you are cooking a small quantity. This recipe makes full use of the microwave but if you don't have one or are adamantly against it, use a shallow sauté pan with a tight-fitting lid instead.

Cut the cabbage into equal halves – you should now have two quartered cabbage head, weighing around 200–250g. Trim the hard core but keep the cabbage joint at the base.

Mix the pork mince with the onion, carrot, ginger, egg yolk, salt and pepper and cornflour together and divide into two equal portions.

With the back of a dessertspoon, spread the pork mixture in between the leaves and tie the cabbage with cooking string. Put the tied cabbage quarters on a microwave-proof dish that is large and deep enough to add the dashi later, cover with clingfilm, prick the clingfilm and microwave for 8 minutes. Take the cabbages out of the dish and set aside. When the cabbages are cool enough to handle, remove the string, cut them into manageable-size pieces and arrange them on serving dishes.

Mix the remaining cornflour with the water. Add the dashi, soy sauce and the cornflour into the dish and microwave for a further 2–3 minutes. Pour the mixture over the cabbages, garnish with the mint leaves and serve.

Okay, so you're feeling peckish. That doesn't surprise me — you're on a diet after all. But I urge you to persevere with *The Chopsticks Diet* because I know that you have nearly reached the goal you set yourself. Here are five recipes that got me through those dark moments when I was feeling hungry and tempted to grab whatever was available. My advice is to make one or two of the recipes when you have spare time, so that you can enjoy some guilt-free, low-calorie healthy snacks to fall back on.

Hunger busters

Spicy konnyaku cubes

Serves 2

- 270g konnyaku
- 1 teaspoon sesame oil
- 3 tablespoons soy sauce
- 1 tablespoon mirin
- ½ teaspoon chilli flakes

Konnyaku (see page 122 to hear about its beneficial properties) must rank very high on the list of 'strange-looking' foods in Japan. It is sold vacuum-packed with limewater and has a long shelf-life if kept in a dark kitchen cupboard. I make a large batch of these snacks and nibble them over a few days whenever I feel peckish.

With your hands, tear the konnyaku into bite-size cubes. Bring a saucepan of water to the boil and poach the konnyaku cubes for 2–3 minutes. Drain and pat dry with kitchen paper.

Place a wok over a high heat, add the oil and stir-fry the konnyaku for 5 minutes.

Reduce the heat to medium, season with the soy sauce and mirin, and continue to cook until almost all the cooking liquid is gone.

Sprinkle with the chilli flakes and transfer to a lidded container to store.

Tip
Don't worry about an uneven, jagged edge on the konnyaku cubes when you prepare them – this increases the surface areas and therefore the flavour.

Kiriboshi daikon instant pickles

Serves 2

- 50g kiriboshi daikon
- 1 deep-fried tofu block
- ½ tablespoon sesame oil
- 125ml Dashi (page 106)
- 1 teaspoon sugar
- 1 tablespoon mirin
- 2 tablespoons soy sauce

Kiriboshi daikon is dried daikon that is rich in various minerals such as natrium, pottasium and calcium. It also contains high levels of edible fibre but above all, it has a deep and comforting sweet taste.

Put the kiriboshi daikon in a large bowl of cold water and rub together to untangle them. Drain and let it stand for 5 minutes to soften before poaching in boiling water for 1 minute. Drain again and when cool enough to handle, chop into manageable-size lengths.

Pour the boiling water over the deep-fried tofu to rid it of excess oil. Cut the tofu in half lengthways and cut into small strips.

Heat the oil in a shallow saucepan over a high heat to coat the kiriboshi daikon and add the tofu. Add the dashi, sugar, mirin and soy sauce then lower the heat to continue cooking while stirring with a pair of cooking chopsticks until almost all the cooking juice is gone. Let it cool down before transferring into a lidded container and eat within three days.

Crunchy rice crisps

Serves 2

- 50g leftover prepared sushi rice (page 132)
- 1 tablespoon toasted black sesame seeds

I have struggled for years to come up with a recipe for leftover sushi rice... and now I proudly present this to you to enjoy.

Preheat the oven to 160°C/325°F/gas mark 3 on a fan-assisted setting. Mix the prepared sushi rice with the sesame seeds and spread on a large sheet of baking parchment.

Sit another sheet on top and roll the rice out to a thin sheet with a rolling pin. Peel off the top parchment. Place the rice sheet in the oven and bake for 10–12 minutes or until it becomes dry and crispy, and browned on the outer edge.

Let it cool down completely and then peel it off the parchment and break into rice crisps. Eat the same day.

Tomato jelly

- 200ml tomato juice
- ½ teaspoon agar agar, diluted in 1 teaspoon water
- 1 teaspoon shredded nori
- a drizzle of balsamic vinegar, (optional)

Here is another use of agar agar to create a healthy and stunning-looking jelly that you can snack on without guilt.

Put the tomato juice in a saucepan with the diluted agar agar. Bring to the boil over a medium heat. Once it starts to boil, reduce the heat to low and cook for 2 minutes.

Turn off the heat, pour it into a mould and let it cool to room temperature before placing it in the fridge to set. Take the jelly out of the mould and garnish with the shredded nori. If you are putting into a container, cut into bite-size cubes and eat within 2 days.

The tomato jelly is particularly nice to eat with a drizzle of vintage balsamic vinegar.

Green tea & soy milk jelly

- 200ml soy milk
- ½ teaspoon agar agar
- 1 teaspoon fruit sugar or sugar
- 1 teaspoon matcha (green tea powder), mixed with 1 tablespoon hot water

Here is a tasty combination of three wonderful diet-friendly foods: green tea, soy milk and agar agar.

Put the soy milk and agar agar powder in a saucepan and bring to the boil. Cook for 2–3 minutes. Add the sugar and dissolved matcha and stir to mix.

Turn off the heat, pour the mixture into a mould and let it cool to room temperature before placing it in the fridge to set.

When it is set, cut into bite-size cubes and eat within two days.

Unlike in western cuisine, where a sweet-flavoured dessert is served at the end of a meal, Japanese cooking does not have desserts after dinner. Instead, a traditional Japanese meal will end on a savoury note with a bowl of rice, served with a bowl of miso soup and a few slices of pickled vegetables. Once the table has been cleared, seasonal fruits may be served along with some cleansing green tea, but these are strictly for 'after the meal'. The Japanese do love their sweets and desserts, especially women and children, but traditional Japanese confectioneries are enjoyed between meals, and most often in the middle of the afternoon with tea.

The health and aesthetic benefits of green teas are widely recognised; catechin, which gives the distinctive astringent taste, is an antioxidant and known to slow down the ageing process, lowers cholesterol and blood pressure, and combined with its high vitamin C content, it is also very good for skin. But much of the beneficial element is non-aqueous and so to get the full advantage you need to 'eat' rather than drink the tea. The practice of eating teas has long existed in China and in Japan, in the form of tea ceremonies where green tea powder is used. I have created a few green-tea themed desserts (along with other low-fat suggestions) to give you guilt-free sweetness to round off your meals.

Desserts

Crème green tea

Serves 2

- 2 teaspoons toasted sesame seeds
- 2 teaspoons match (green tea powder)
- 2 tablespoons brown sugar
- 200ml soy milk
- 1/2 teaspoon agar agar
- 2 raspberries

In this recipe, green tea, agar agar and soy milk are brought together to create a delicious, healthy, guilt-free dessert. Agar agar is a type of seaweed that is not dissimilar to gelatine but it is vegetarian and has a much greater ability to set. It has no calories, is rich in minerals, notably iron and calcium, and has an incredible amount of edible fibre so it leaves you feeling satisfied for a long time. Agar agar is also known to help to lower cholesterol, blood pressure and body fat — altogether it is an ideal ingredient for healthy weight loss!

Put the sesame seeds in a mortar and grind with the pestle until smooth. Add the matcha and brown sugar and continue to grind until the mixture becomes uniform and smooth.

Dissolve the agar agar in a little bowl with a tablespoon of the soy milk. In a heatproof bowl, mix the rest of the soy milk with the tea mixture and add the agar agar. Cover the bowl with a piece of clingfilm and microwave on medium for 90 seconds, stirring a couple of times.

Remove the clingfilm and pour it into two serving glasses. Let them cool to room temperature and then refrigerate. Place a raspberry in the centre of each glass and serve. (For three servings, see picture, multiply the quantities by a third.)

Watermelon cubes

Serves 2

- 400g watermelon, skinned
- 2 tablespoons white sesame seeds
- 2 tablespoons black sesame seeds

This is a refreshing and delicious way to eat watermelon.

Deseed the watermelon. Cut into bite-size cubes.

Put the white and black sesame seeds on separate plates. Dip one side of the watermelon cubes into the seeds and serve with chopsticks.

Green tea sorbet

Serves 2

- 200ml water
- 3 tablespoons sugar
- 2 teaspoons matcha (green tea powder), mixed with 2 tablespoons hot water

Sorbet is the perfect ice-cream substitute for slimmers.

Put the water and sugar in a saucepan to heat until all the sugar is dissolved. Add the dilssolved matcha and mix well to incorporate. Pour into an ice tray.

When it has cooled to room temperature, put the tray in the freezer for 30 minutes or until the edges begin to ice.

With a fork, stir to fluff up the semi-ice and return to the freezer to continue freezing until desired.